Mathscheck

ASSESSMENT PAPERS FOR NATIONAL CURRICULUM MATHEMATICS

WORKING TOWARDS LEVEL DESCRIPTION

4

Paul Harling

Collins Educational
An Imprint of HarperCollins*Publishers*

Second edition
Fully revised

Published by Collins Educational
77– 85 Fulham Palace Road
London W6 8JB

An imprint of HarperCollins Publishers
© HarperCollins Publishers Ltd

First published 1993

Reprinted 1994

Second edition 1996

ISBN 0 00 312653 6

Edited by: John Day

Designed, produced and illustrated by: Gecko Ltd, Bicester, Oxon

Printed by: Martins Printers, Berwick-upon-Tweed

Mathscheck

AT   Level Description and Test Focus

Ma2   *Pupils use their understanding of place value to multiply and divide whole numbers by 10 or 100. In solving number problems, pupils use a range of mental and written methods of computation with the four operations, including mental recall of multiplication facts up to 10 × 10. They add and subtract decimals to two places. In solving problems with or without a calculator, pupils check the reasonableness of their results by reference to their knowledge of the context or to the size of the numbers. They recognise approximate proportions of a whole and use simple fractions and percentages to describe these. Pupils explore and describe number patterns, and relationships including multiple, factor and square. They have begun to use simple formulae expressed in words. Pupils use and interpret co-ordinates in the first quadrant.*

		Series 1	2	Answer sheets
Test 1	Place value. Multiplying & dividing by 10 or 100	23–24	57–58	92–93
Test 2	Mental recall of multiplication facts to 10 × 10	25	59	94
Test 3	Adding numbers with up to three digits	26	60	95
Test 4	Subtracting numbers with up to three digits	27	61	96
Test 5	Multiplying numbers up to 100 by single-digit numbers	28	62	97
Test 6	Dividing numbers up to 100 by single-digit numbers	29	63	98
Test 7	Adding decimals to two places	30	64	99
Test 8	Subtracting decimals to two places	31	65	100
Test 9	Rounding & approximating. Interpreting calculator displays	32–33	66–67	101–102
Test 10	Fractions & percentages to describe proportions	34	68	103
Test 11	Number patterns & related terminology	35–37	69–71	104–106
Test 12	Using simple formulae expressed in words	38–40	72–74	107–109
Test 13	Using & interpreting co-ordinates in the first quadrant	41	75	110

Mathscheck

What is Mathscheck?

Mathscheck is a comprehensive set of photocopiable test papers and schedules which can be used to monitor pupils' progress through the National Curriculum for mathematics. The materials are fully referenced to the National Curriculum Programmes of Study and Level Descriptions which were introduced in the 1995 National Curriculum orders. *Mathscheck* is designed to be used as part of normal classwork, providing you with supportive documentation to complement both continuous assessment and the statutory end-of-key-stage assessment.

Purposes of *Mathscheck*

Mathscheck enables you to:

- Compare pupils' performance with the levels prescribed by the National Curriculum.

- Identify the particular strengths and weaknesses of pupils so that teaching can be structured to meet the needs of individuals and groups.

- Group pupils in different ways for the teaching and learning of various aspects of the mathematics curriculum.

- Gain an overall picture of pupils' progress so that you can devise long- and short-term teaching strategies.

- Gather evidence on which to base discussion of pupils' attainments with pupils, colleagues and parents.

- Provide evidence when recording and reporting pupils' attainments.

- Decide more easily which levels of statutory Standard Tasks are appropriate for a pupil.

Mathscheck and the National Curriculum

Programmes of Study and Level Descriptions

Within the National Curriculum the Programme of Study (PoS) for each Key Stage is the tool for curriculum planning, setting out the required breadth and depth of learning of mathematical content. *Mathscheck* has used the PoS to determine the content and style of each test.

The Level Descriptions form the heart of assessment within the National Curriculum. They provide basic objectives or criteria against which pupils' progress can be monitored. They *indicate* what 'pupils working at a particular level should characteristically demonstrate'. They are designed to be used holistically, at the end of each Key Stage, as guidance in reporting a pupil's progress. With this in mind 'a pupil's performance in relation to Level Descriptions should be considered in conjunction with the Description for adjacent Levels'.

The *Mathscheck* test papers are written to allow you easily to assess pupils' attainment in small sections of mathematics as they take part in normal classwork. The Level Descriptions clearly indicate a sense of progression through National Curriculum mathematics; for that reason the sequence of the *Mathscheck* tests follows the order set out in the statutory Level Descriptions. Each test is cross-referenced with the statutory Level Descriptions (pages 5–6) and the appropriate Programme of Study for each Key Stage (pages 7–19).

Attainment Targets

The National Curriculum sets out various stages in the growth of mathematical understanding, specifying eight levels of achievement across four Attainment Targets.

Attainment Target 1 (Ma 1): Using and Applying Mathematics
This Attainment Target is assessed at every Key Stage.

1

Attainment Target 2 (Ma 2): Number and Algebra
For the purposes of National Curriculum assessment, Number and Algebra are listed as a single Attainment Target, with one set of Level Descriptions. However, in Key Stages 1 and 2 the relevant section of the Programme of Study is referred to as Number. In the Programme of Study for Key Stages 3 and 4, Number and Algebra are listed separately.

Attainment Target 3 (Ma 3): Shape, Space and Measures
This Attainment Target is assessed separately at every Key Stage, although a few aspects of measurement are included within Attainment Target 2: Number and Algebra.

Attainment Target 4 (Ma 4): Handling Data
In the Programme of Study for Key Stage 1 elements of content related to Handling Data are subsumed under the Number section. However, the Level Descriptions relating to Handling Data include criteria for attainment at Levels 1 and 2. Therefore, to provide you with consistency and sequence in the assessment of concepts *Mathscheck* offers assessment items for Handling Data at Key Stage 1 as separate tests.

It should be noted that the Level Descriptions do not apply to Key Stage 4. The *Mathscheck* series contains a separate book of materials to assess 'exceptional performance' in which pupils' attainment is 'beyond Level 8'.

The *Mathscheck* materials

Levels

The tests and checklists are presented in separate books for pupils working towards each of the Level Descriptions, although Levels 1 and 2 are combined. Within each book the tests are arranged in blocks related to each Attainment Target. Within each block the order of the tests follows the usual progression of learning of an average pupil.

Parallel forms

There are parallel tests for each assessment, referred to as *Series 1* and *Series 2*. This allows for re-testing, or for pupils to work on different test items for the same mathematical content in one class.

Test content

The heading for each test clearly references that test to the National Curriculum. It shows: Attainment Target and Level; a brief description of the content 'focus' of the test; the element of the Level Description to which it relates; and the test series (1 or 2).

Using and applying mathematics

Attainment Target 1 (Ma 1) is different from the other three Attainment Targets. Whereas Ma 2 to Ma 4 describe progression in knowledge, skills and understanding, Attainment Target 1 is concerned with use and application of that knowledge and understanding, and those skills.

In the 1995 Orders the rubric of the Programme of Study for Key Stage 1 states:

> The sections of the programme of study interrelate. Developing mathematical language, selecting and using materials, and developing reasoning, should be set in the context of the other areas of mathematics.

Similarly the advice for Key Stages 3 and 4 states that:

> Using mathematics, communicating mathematically and reasoning should be set in the context of the other areas of mathematics.

The wide ranging purpose of Ma 1 suggests that pencil-and-paper tests are inappropriate. What is needed is a broad overview of a pupil's performance in Ma 1 across the whole range of mathematical work. *Mathscheck* contains carefully researched checklists of 'average behaviours' of pupils who are effectively 'using and applying' mathematics at each level of attainment. Regular completion of relevant parts of the checklists after observation of, and discussion with, pupils provides systematic evidence to complement your own assessments.

If a pupil is achieving most of the specified items at a given level, while working mathematically on the content and skills in Ma 2–Ma 4, then you can be confident that he or she is working successfully at that level in Ma 1. To allow for variations in pupils' skills in Ma 1, and to highlight the sense of progression, the checklists of the levels immediately above and below the designated level are included in each book.

The Ma 1 checklists are on pages 20–22.

Using the *Mathscheck* materials

When to use Mathscheck

Mathscheck has been designed to be used as part of your continuous assessment of pupil attainment and progress. Therefore the tests should be used on an ad hoc basis – not in a block at the end of a term or year.

Building evidence

The results of the tests provide evidence on a continuous basis. Simple record sheets are provided (pages 5–6) for recording the date of satisfactory completion of each test and also for indicating which element of a Level Description has been met by a pupil.

Equipment

The test sheets include space for working. For the majority of the tests there are no special equipment needs. However, in a very few cases, you will need to set up a simple practical situation or provide a computer or calculator. These needs are highlighted in the notes (page 4), which should be read before using any of the tests in the pack.

Time limits

We have not written the tests with any time limits in mind. Pupils should be given the time that they need to fully demonstrate their knowledge and skill.

Marking

Facsimile pages containing the answers are provided on pages 92–125.

Reading out the questions

Some of the tests lend themselves to being read out to the pupils. This is particularly true of the lower-level tests. Where the National Curriculum requires pupils to read the instructions for themselves the general notes for each book again make this clear. In general, reading requirements have been kept to a minimum.

Special educational needs

The tests are related to Levels rather than ages or year groups and can be cut-and-pasted in any form. This may be useful for slower pupils who may be overwhelmed by a full page of activities.

What constitutes 'attainment'?

The decision about whether a pupil has attained a level depends on your judgement as the teacher. However, for each test, you should require correct responses to at least 75% of the items on the test if you are to credit the pupil with success.

Following-up the testing process

Pupils should be encouraged to discuss what has been achieved on a test, to confirm progress or to highlight aspects of their work which need more experience or practice. In this way the assessment process becomes 'formative' and provides excellent practice material to prepare pupils for the end-of-key-stage statutory assessments.

With this in mind it is useful to:

● Show pupils how they can lose marks through simple carelessness. Pupils should be encouraged to read the tasks carefully and to ask for clarification if in any doubt about what they are being asked to do.

● Remind pupils that a good deal of mathematics requires them to have memorised basic facts and techniques. They can be shown how practising techniques can be a key to success. Often a small hint may be enough to remind them of something they actually know.

● Clearly highlight the concepts, skills or processes which seem to have been misunderstood, with a suggestion about planning for further experience.

● Discuss the differences in style and wording of 'questions' in various published materials used in the classroom. A pupil may simply be unfamiliar with the type of task and what it requires. *Mathscheck* includes a wide range of types and styles of task or question.

● Provide pupils with experience of more than one way to approach a calculation or a problem, allowing 'informal' methods to be used when appropriate. *Mathscheck* encourages practice in 'reading' the mathematics and interpreting questions in the most suitable way – an essential skill.

Paul Harling
September 1995

Notes for Level 4

Please read this page before using the assessment sheets

Test 1	Pupils should not use a calculator. There should be no evidence of 'working out' the answers since the questions require mental arithmetic. However, it would be appropriate to ask the pupil to explain verbally how the answer is reached.
Test 2	This test requires mental recall only, and can be delivered orally if appropriate to the class.
Test 3	Pupils should not use a calculator. The test is carefully sequenced to allow assessment and diagnosis of basic addition skills. Observation of the pupil's ability to use skills in various contexts is also recommended.
Test 4	Pupils should not use a calculator. The test is carefully sequenced to allow assessment and diagnosis of basic subtraction skills. Observation of the pupil's ability to use the skills in various contexts is also recommended.
Test 5	Pupils should not use a calculator. The test is carefully sequenced to allow assessment and diagnosis of basic multiplication skills. Observation of the pupil's ability to use the skills in various contexts is also recommended.
Test 6	Pupils should not use a calculator. The test is carefully sequenced to allow assessment and diagnosis of basic division skills. Observation of the pupil's ability to use the skills in various contexts is also recommended.
Test 7	Pupils should not use a calculator. The test is carefully sequenced to allow assessment and diagnosis of the basic skills of adding decimals. Observation of the pupil's ability to use the skills in various contexts is also recommended.
Test 8	Pupils should not use a calculator. The test is carefully sequenced to allow assessment and diagnosis of the basic skills of subtracting decimals. Observation of the pupil's ability to use the skills in various contexts is also recommended.
Test 9	A calculator is required for some questions. Oral follow-up is recommended to ensure appropriatenesss of the pupil's reasoning.
Test 10	The emphasis of the test is on describing situations. Calculations are assessed in later levels.
Test 11	It is important the pupil's responses are discussed during the assessment, or subsequently.
Test 12	It is important the pupil's responses are discussed during the assessment, or subsequently.
Test 13	The tasks in this test can be linked to Ma3 by asking the pupils to name and describe the shape produced.
Test 14	The appropriate equipment needs to be available in advance of the assessment.
Test 15	The test includes selected skills of constructing and analysing 2-D shapes and can be completed as part of general classwork in shape.
Test 16	Tracing paper should be available so that pupils can check their predictions.
Test 17	This is essentially a practical element and the assessment will highlight potential problems to be worked on in a practical context.
Test 18	Apparatus should be available to those pupils who need support.
Test 19	Apparatus should be available to those pupils who need support.
Test 20	This test can be adapted to suit the needs of any cross-curricular context requiring handling of data.
Test 21	This test can be adapted to suit the needs of any cross-curricular context requiring handling of data.
Test 22	This test can be adapted to suit the needs of any cross-curricular context requiring handling of data.
Test 23	This test can be adapted to suit the needs of any cross-curricular context requiring handling of data.
Test 24	At this level probability is essentially about understanding terms and simple concepts of uncertainty. Oral follow-up is recommended.

Name _____ **Date of birth** _____

National Curriculum Level Record

Write the date of attainment of each element of the Level Descriptions and comment as appropriate

	Level Description	*Mathscheck* Links	Date	Comments
Ma1 Using and applying maths	Pupils: ● are developing their own strategies for solving problems and are using these strategies both in working within mathematics and in applying mathematics to practical contexts ● present information and results in a clear and organised way, explaining the reason for their presentation ● search for a pattern by trying out ideas of their own	Refer to the checklist on page 21		
Ma2 Number and algebra	Pupils: ● use their understanding of place value to multiply and divide whole numbers by 10 or 100 ● [in solving number problems] use a range of mental and written methods of computation with the four operations, including mental recall of multiplication facts up to 10×10 ● add and subtract decimals to two places ● [in solving problems with or without a calculator] check the reasonableness of their results by reference to their knowledge of the context or to the size of the numbers ● recognise approximate proportions of a whole and use simple fractions and percentages to describe these ● explore and describe number patterns, and relationships including multiple, factor and square ● have begun to use simple formulae expressed in words ● use and interpret co-ordinates in the first quadrant	Tests 1 2 3 4 5 6 7 8 9 10 11 12 13		

	Level Description	*Mathscheck* Links	Date	Comments
Ma3 Shape, space and measures	Pupils ● make 3-D mathematical models by linking given faces or edges, draw common 2-D shapes in different orientations on grids, and identify congruent shapes and orders of rotational symmetry ● reflect simple shapes in a mirror line ● choose and use appropriate units and instruments, interpreting, with appropriate accuracy, numbers on a range of measuring instruments ● find perimeters of simple shapes, find areas by counting squares, and find volumes by counting cubes	Tests 14 15 16 17 18 19		
Ma4 Handling data	Pupils: ● collect discrete data and record them using a frequency table ● understand and use the mode and median ● group data, where appropriate, in equal class intervals, represent collected data in frequency diagrams and interpret such diagrams ● construct and interpret simple line graphs ● understand and use simple vocabulary associated with probability, including 'fair', 'certain' and 'likely'	Tests 20 21 22 23 24		

Mathscheck and the Programme of Study for Key Stage 1

	National Curriculum Levels and *Mathscheck* Tests		
Using and Applying Mathematics	1	2	3
1 Pupils should be given opportunities to: *a* use and apply mathematics in practical tasks, in real-life problems and within mathematics itself; *b* explain their thinking to support the development of their reasoning.	| *This section outlines some general aims and required approaches of the Attainment Target.*		
2 Making and monitoring decisions to solve problems Pupils should be taught to: *a* select and use the appropriate mathematics; *b* select and use mathematical equipment and materials; *c* develop different mathematical approaches and look for ways to overcome difficulties; *d* organise and check their work.	*Refer to the criteria for successful attainment given in Levels 1 & 2, page 14.*	*Refer to the criteria for successful attainment given in Levels 1 & 2, page 15; in Level 3, page 19.*	*Refer to the criteria for successful attainment given on page 20; in Levels 1 & 2, page 16; in Level 3, page 20.*
3 Developing mathematical language and communication Pupils should be taught to: *a* understand the language of number, properties of shapes and comparatives, eg *'bigger than'*, *'next to'*, *'before'*; *b* relate numerals and other mathematical symbols, eg '+', '=', to a range of situations; *c* discuss their work, responding to and asking mathematical questions; *d* use a variety of forms of mathematical presentation.			
4 Developing mathematical reasoning Pupils should be taught to: *a* recognise simple patterns and relationships and make related predictions about them; *b* ask questions including 'What would happen if?' and 'Why?', eg *considering the behaviour of a programmable toy*; *c* understand general statements, eg *'all even numbers divide by 2'*, and investigate whether particular cases match them.			
Number	1	2	3
1 Pupils should be given opportunities to: *a* develop flexible methods of working with number, orally and mentally; *b* encounter numbers greater than 1000; *c* use a variety of practical resources and contexts; *d* use calculators both as a means to explore number and as a tool for calculating with realistic data, eg *numbers with several digits*; *e* record in a variety of ways, including ways that relate to their mental work; *f* use computer software, including a database.	*This section outlines some general aims and required approaches of the Attainment Target.*		
2 Developing an understanding of place value Pupils should be taught to: *a* count orally up to 10 and beyond, knowing the number names; count collections of objects, checking the total; count in steps of different sizes, eg *count on from 5 in steps of 2 or 3*; recognise sequences, including odd and even numbers;	1	1, 2, 3, 4	1, 4, 5
b read, write and order numbers, initially to 10, progressing up to 1000, developing an understanding that the position of a digit signifies its value; begin to approximate large numbers to the nearest 10 or 100;	1, 4	1, 2	1, 2, 7, 8

Number (continued)	1	2	3

National Curriculum Levels and *Mathscheck* Tests

	1	2	3
c recognise and use in context simple fractions, including halves and quarters, decimal notation in recording money, and negative numbers, eg *a temperature scale, a number line, a calculator display*.		3	3, 5

3 Understanding relationships between numbers and developing methods of computation
Pupils should be taught to:

	1	2	3
a use repeating patterns to develop ideas of regularity and sequencing;	4	4	8
b explore and record patterns in addition and subtraction, and then patterns of multiples, eg *3, 6, 9, 12*, explaining their patterns and using them to make predictions; progress to exploring further patterns involving multiplication and division, including those within a hundred-square of multiplication facts;		1, 4	4, 7, 8
c know addition and subtraction facts to 20, and develop a range of methods for finding, from known facts, those that they cannot recall; learn multiplication and division facts relating to the 2s, 5s, 10s, and use these to learn other facts, eg *double multiples of 2 to produce multiples of 4*, and to develop mental methods for finding new results;	2, 3	1, 2, 4	3, 4, 5, 7, 8
d develop a variety of methods for adding and subtracting, including using the fact that subtraction is the inverse of addition;	2, 3	1, 2, 4	1, 3, 7, 8
e use a basic calculator, reading the display, eg *use the constant function to explore repeated addition*.			3, 5

4 Solving numerical problems
Pupils should be taught to:

	1	2	3
a understand the operations of addition, subtraction as taking away and comparison, and the relationship between them, recognise situations to which they apply and use them to solve problems with whole numbers, including situations involving money;	2, 3	1, 2, 4	1, 3, 7, 8
b understand the operations of multiplication, and division as sharing and repeated subtraction, and use them to solve problems with whole numbers or money, understanding and dealing appropriately with remainders;		3	4, 5, 6
c choose a suitable method of computation, using apparatus where appropriate, or a calculator where the numbers include several digits;	2, 3	1, 2, 4	1, 4, 5, 8
d begin to check answers in different ways, eg *repeating the calculation in a different order or using a different method*, and gain a feel for the appropriate size of an answer.	2, 3	1, 2, 4	1, 2, 4, 5, 8

5 Classifying, representing and interpreting data
Pupils should be taught to:

	1	2	3
a sort and classify a set of objects using criteria related to their properties, eg *size, shape, mass*;	5, 7, 9	5, 8	9, 10, 11
b collect, record and interpret data arising from an area of interest, using an increasing range of charts, diagrams, tables and graphs.		8, 9	16, 17, 18

Shape, Space and Measures	1	2	3

1 Pupils should be given opportunities to:

a gain a wide range of practical experiences using a variety of materials;	*This section outlines some general aims and required approaches of the Attainment Target.*
b use IT devices, eg *programmable toys, turtle graphics packages*;	
c use purposeful contexts for measuring.	

Shape, Space and Measures (continued)	National Curriculum Levels and *Mathscheck* Tests		
	1	2	3
2 Understanding and using patterns and properties of shape Pupils should be taught to:			
a describe and discuss shapes and patterns that can be seen or visualised;	5	5	9, 10, 11
b make common 3-D and 2-D shapes and models, working with increasing care and accuracy; begin to classify shapes according to mathematical criteria;	5	5	9, 10, 11, 12
c recognise and use the geometrical features of shapes, including vertices, sides/edges and surfaces, rectangles (including squares), circles, triangles, cubes, cuboids, progressing to hexagons, pentagons, cylinders and spheres; recognise reflective symmetry in simple cases.	5	5	9, 10, 11, 12
3 Understanding and using properties of position and movement Pupils should be taught to:			
a describe positions, using common words; recognise movements in a straight line, ie translations, and rotations, and combine them in simple ways; copy, continue and make patterns;	6	6	9, 10, 11, 12
b understand angle as a measure of turn and recognise quarter-turns and half-turns, eg *giving instructions for rotating a programmable toy*; recognise right angles.		5, 6	9, 10
4 Understanding and using measures Pupils should be taught to:			
a compare objects and events using appropriate language, by direct comparison, and then using common non-standard and standard units of length, mass and capacity, eg *'three-and-a-bit metres long'*, *'as heavy as ten conkers'*, *'about three beakers full'*; begin to use a wider range of standard units, including standard units of time, choosing units appropriate to a situation; estimate with these units;	7, 8	7	13, 14, 15
b choose and use simple measuring instruments, reading and interpreting numbers and scales with some accuracy.		7	13, 14, 15

Mathscheck and the Programme of Study for Key Stage 2

	National Curriculum Levels and *Mathscheck* Tests			
Using and Applying Mathematics	2	3	4	5
1 Pupils should be given opportunities to: *a* use and apply mathematics in practical tasks, in real-life problems and within mathematics itself; *b* take increasing responsibility for organising and extending tasks; *c* devise and refine their own ways of recording; *d* ask questions and follow alternative suggestions to support the development of reasoning.	*This section outlines some general aims and required approaches of the Attainment Target.*			

2 Making and monitoring decisions to solve problems
Pupils should be taught to:
 	
a select and use the appropriate mathematics and materials;
 	
b try different mathematical approaches; identify and obtain information needed to carry out their work;
 	
c develop their own mathematical strategies and look for ways to overcome difficulties;
 	
d check their results and consider whether they are reasonable.
 	
3 Developing mathematical language and forms of communication
Pupils should be taught to:
 	
a understand and use the language of:
  number;
  the properties and movements of shapes;
  measures;
  simple probability;
  relationships, including 'multiple of', 'factor of' and 'symmetrical to';
 	
b use diagrams, graphs and simple algebraic symbols;
 	
c present information and results clearly, and explain the reasons for their choice of presentation.
 	
4 Developing mathematical reasoning
Pupils should be taught to:
 	
a understand and investigate general statements, eg *'wrist size is half neck size'*, *'there are four prime numbers less than 10'*;
 	
b search for pattern in their results;
 	
c make general statements of their own, based on evidence they have produced;
 	
d explain their reasoning.
	Refer to the criteria for successful attainment given in Levels 1&2, page 15; in Level 3, page 19.	*Refer to the criteria for successful attainment given on page 20; in Levels 1&2, page 16; in Level 3, page 20.*	*Refer to the criteria for successful attainment given on page 21; in Level 3, page 21; in Level 5, page 17*	*Refer to the criteria for successful attainment given on page 22; in Level 5, page 18; in Level 6, page 13.*

Number	2	3	4	5
1 Pupils should be given opportunities to: *a* develop flexible and effective methods of computation and recording, and use them with understanding; *b* use calculators, computers and a range of other resources as tools for exploring number structure and to enable work with realistic data; *c* develop the skills needed for accurate and appropriate use of equipment.	*This section outlines some general aims and required approaches of the Attainment Target.*			

Number (continued)	National Curriculum Levels and *Mathscheck* Tests			
	2	3	4	5
2 Developing an understanding of place value and extending the number system Pupils should be taught to:				
a read, write and order whole numbers, understanding that the position of a digit signifies its value; use their understanding of place value to develop methods of computation, to approximate numbers to the nearest 10 or 100, and to multiply and divide by powers of 10 when there are whole-number answers;	1, 2	1, 2, 5	1, 3, 4, 5, 6, 7, 8, 9	1,5
b extend their understanding of the number system to negative numbers in context, and decimals with no more than two decimal places in the context of measurement and money;		3, 5	7, 8, 9	1, 2, 3, 9
c understand and use, in context, fractions and percentages to estimate, describe and compare proportions of a whole.	3		10	4
3 Understanding relationships between numbers and developing methods of computation Pupils should be taught to:				
a explore number sequences eg *counting in different sizes of step, doubling and halving, using a multiplication square*, explaining patterns and using simple relationships; progress to interpreting, generalising and using simple mappings, eg *C = 15n for the cost of n articles at 15p*, relating to numerical, spatial or practical situations, expressed initially in words and then using letters as symbols;	1, 4	4, 8	11, 12	6
b recognise the number relationship between co-ordinates in the first quadrant of related points on a line or in a shape, eg *the vertices of a rectangle, a graph of the multiples of 3*;			13	
c consolidate knowledge of addition and subtraction facts to 20; know the multiplication facts to 10 × 10; develop a range of mental methods for finding quickly from known facts those that they cannot recall; use some properties of numbers, including multiples, factors and squares, extending to primes, cubes and square roots;	1, 2, 4	1, 3, 4, 5, 7	1, 2, 5, 6, 9, 11, 12	3
d develop a variety of mental methods of computation with whole numbers up to 100, and explain patterns used; extend mental methods to develop a range of non-calculator methods of computation that involve addition and subtraction of whole numbers, progressing to methods for multiplication and division of up to three-digit by two-digit whole numbers;	1, 2, 4	1, 3, 5, 7, 8	1, 3, 4, 5, 6, 11, 12	1, 3, 5
e understand multiplication as repeated addition, and division as sharing and repeated subtraction; use associated language and recognise situations to which the operations apply;	3	4, 5, 6	1, 2, 5, 6, 12	3, 5
f understand and use the relationships between the four operations, including inverses;	1, 2, 4	4, 5, 8	1, 3, 4, 5 6, 9, 12	1, 3, 5
g extend methods of computation to include addition and subtraction with negative numbers, all four operations with decimals, and calculating fractions and percentages of quantities, using a calculator where appropriate;		3, 5	7, 8, 9, 10	3, 4
h understand and use the features of a basic calculator, interpreting the display in the context of the problem, including rounding and remainders.		3, 5, 6	9	4

Number (continued)	National Curriculum Levels and *Mathscheck* Tests			
	2	**3**	**4**	**5**
4 Solving numerical problems Pupils should be taught to:				
a develop their use of the four operations to solve problems, including those involving money and measures, using a calculator where appropriate;	1, 2, 4	3, 4, 5, 8	1, 2, 3, 4, 5, 6, 7, 8, 11, 12	3, 5
b choose sequences of methods of computation appropriate to a problem, adapt them and apply them accurately;	1, 2, 4	3, 4, 5, 8	1, 2, 3, 4, 5, 6, 7, 8, 11, 12	1, 3, 5
c check results by different methods, including repeating the operations in a different order or using inverse operations; gain a sense of the size of a solution, and estimate and approximate solutions to problems.	1, 2, 4	1, 3, 4, 5, 7, 8	1, 2, 3, 4, 5, 6, 7, 8, 9, 11, 12	1, 3, 5

Shape, Space and Measures	**2**	**3**	**4**	**5**
1 Pupils should be given opportunities to:				
a use geometrical properties and relationships in the solution of problems;				
b extend their practical experience using a wide range of materials;		*This section outlines some general aims and required approaches of the Attainment Target.*		
c use computers to create and transform shapes;				
d consider a wide range of patterns, including some drawn from different cultural traditions;				
e apply their measuring skills in a range of purposeful contexts.				
2 Understanding and using properties of shape Pupils should be taught to:				
a visualise and describe shapes and movements, developing precision in using related geometrical language;	5	9, 10, 11, 12	14, 15, 16	7, 8
b make 2-D and 3-D shapes and patterns with increasing accuracy, recognise their geometrical features and properties, and use these to classify shapes and solve problems;	5	9, 10, 11, 12	14, 15, 16	7, 8
c understand the congruence of simple shapes; recognise reflective symmetries of 2-D and 3-D shapes, and rotational symmetries of 2-D shapes.	6	12	15, 16, 17	8
3 Understanding and using properties of position and movement Pupils should be taught to:				
a transform 2-D shapes by translation, reflection and rotation, and visualise movements and simple transformations to create and describe patterns;	5, 6	12	16, 17	7, 8
b use co-ordinates to specify location, eg *map references, representation of 2-D shapes*;			13	
c use right angles, fractions of a turn and, later, degrees, to measure rotation, and use the associated language.	5, 6	9	15	7

Shape, Space and Measures *(continued)*	National Curriculum Levels and *Mathscheck* Tests			
	2	**3**	**4**	**5**
4 Understanding and using measures Pupils should be taught to:				
a choose appropriate standard units of length, mass, capacity and time, and make sensible estimates with them in everyday situations; extend their understanding of the relationship between units; convert one metric unit to another; know the rough metric equivalents of Imperial units still in daily use;	7	13, 14, 15	18	9, 10
b choose and use appropriate measuring instruments; interpret numbers and read scales to an increasing degree of accuracy;	7	13, 14, 15	18	10
c find perimeters of simple shapes; find practically the circumferences of circles, being introduced to the ratio π; find areas and volumes by counting methods, leading to the use of other practical methods, eg *dissection*.			19	6

Handling Data†	2	3	4	5
1 Pupils should be given opportunities to:				
a formulate questions about an issue of their choice, and consider them using statistical methods;	*This section outlines some general aims and required approaches of the Attainment Target.*			
b access and collect data through undertaking purposeful enquiries;				
c use computers as a source of interesting data, and as a tool for representing data.				
2 Collecting, representing and interpreting data Pupils should be taught to:				
a interpret tables used in everyday life; interpret and create frequency tables, including those for grouped discrete data;	8, 9	16, 17, 18	20, 22, 23	11, 12
b collect and represent discrete data appropriately using graphs and diagrams, including block graphs, pictograms and line graphs; interpret a wider range of graphs and diagrams that represent data, including pie charts, using a computer where appropriate;	9	16, 17, 18	20, 23	11, 12, 13
c understand and use measures of average, leading towards the mode, the median and the mean in relevant contexts, and the range as a measure of spread;			21, 22	11
d draw conclusions from statistics and graphs, and recognise why some conclusions can be uncertain or misleading.	9	16, 17, 18	20, 21, 22, 23	11, 13
3 Understanding and using probability Pupils should be taught to:				
a develop understanding of probability, through experience as well as experiment and theory, and discuss events and simple experiments, using a vocabulary that includes the words 'evens', 'fair', 'unfair', 'certain', 'likely', 'probably', and 'equally likely';			24	14
b understand that the probability of any event lies between impossibility and certainty, leading to the use of the scale from 0 to 1;				14, 15
c recognise situations where probabilities can be based on equally likely outcomes, and others where estimates must be based on experimental evidence; make or approximate these estimates.			24	14, 15

† At Key Stage 1, this Attainment Target is subsumed under Number.

Mathscheck and the Programme of Study for Key Stages 3 and 4

National Curriculum Levels and Mathscheck Tests

	3	4	5	6	7	8
	This section outlines some general aims and required approaches of the Attainment Target.					
Level 8						*Refer to the criteria for successful attainment given in Level 7, page 15; in Level 8, page 14.*
Level 7					*Refer to the criteria for successful attainment given in Level 6, page 15; in Level 7, page 14; in Level 8, page 13.*	
Level 6				*Refer to the criteria for successful attainment given in Level 5, page 19; in Level 6, page 14; in Level 7, page 13.*		
Level 5			*Refer to the criteria for successful attainment given in Level 4, page 22; in Level 5, page 18; in Level 6, page 13.*			
Level 4		*Refer to the criteria for successful attainment given on page 21; in Level 3, page 21; in Level 5, page 17.*				
Level 3	*Refer to the criteria for successful attainment given on page 20; in Levels 1&2, page 16; in Level 3, page 20.*					

Using and Applying Mathematics

1 Pupils should be given opportunities to:

a use and apply mathematics in practical tasks, in real-life problems and within mathematics itself;

b work on problems that pose a challenge;

c encounter and consider different lines of mathematical argument.

2 Making and monitoring decisions to solve problems
Pupils should be taught to:

a find ways of overcoming difficulties that arise; develop and use their own strategies;

b select, trial and evaluate a variety of possible approaches; identify what further information may be required in order to pursue a particular line of enquiry; break complex problems into a series of tasks;

c select and organise mathematics and resources; extend their work to related tasks; select, follow and reflect on alternative approaches of their own;

d review progress whilst engaging in work, and check and evaluate solutions.

3 Communicating mathematically
Pupils should be taught to:

a understand and use mathematical language and notation;

b use mathematical forms of communication, including diagrams, tables, graphs and computer print-outs;

c present work clearly, using diagrams, graphs and symbols appropriately, to convey meaning;

d interpret mathematics presented in a variety of forms; evaluate forms of presentation;

e examine critically, improve and justify their choice of mathematical presentation.

4 Developing skills of mathematical reasoning
Pupils should be taught to:

a explain and justify how they arrived at a conclusion or solution to a problem;

b make conjectures and hypotheses, designing methods to test them, and analysing results to see whether they are valid;

c understand general statements, leading to making and testing generalisations; recognise particular examples, and appreciate the difference between mathematical explanation and experimental evidence;

d appreciate and use 'if... then...' lines of argument in number, algebra and geometry, and draw inferences from statistics;

e use mathematical reasoning, initially when explaining, and then when following a line of argument, recognising inconsistencies.

Number	3	4	5	6	7	8
National Curriculum Levels and _Mathscheck_ Tests						
1 Pupils should be given opportunities to:						
_a_ use calculators and computer software, eg _spreadsheets;_	_This section outlines some general aims and required approaches of the Attainment Target._					
_b_ develop and use flexibly a range of methods of computation, and apply these to a range of problems.						
2 Understanding place value and extending the number system Pupils should be taught to:						
_a_ understand and use the concept of place value in whole numbers and decimals; relating this to computation and the metric system of measurement;	1, 3, 13, 14, 15	1, 7, 8, 9	1, 3	1, 2	1	
_b_ understand and use decimals, ratios, fractions and percentages, and the interrelationships between them; understand and use negative numbers;	3	7, 8, 9, 10	1, 2, 3	3, 4	5	3
_c_ understand and use index notation, leading to standard form.						1, 2
3 Understanding and using relationships between numbers and developing methods of computation Pupils should be taught to:						
_a_ consolidate knowledge of number facts, including multiplication to 10 × 10, developing use of methods for finding quickly from known facts those that they cannot recall; use some common properties of numbers, including multiples, factors and primes, leading to powers and roots;	1, 4, 5, 7	1, 2, 3, 4, 5, 6, 11	1, 5	2		1
_b_ extend mental methods of computation, to consolidate a range of non-calculator methods of addition and subtraction of whole numbers, and multiplication and division of whole numbers by whole numbers, understanding and using accurately the methods that they choose;	4, 5, 6, 7, 8	1, 2, 3, 4, 5, 6	1, 5		1	2
_c_ calculate with negative numbers, decimals, fractions, percentages and ratio, understanding the effects of operations, eg _squaring, multiplying and dividing by numbers between 0 and 1,_ and selecting an appropriate non-calculator or calculator method;		7, 8, 10	2, 3, 4	1, 2, 3, 4	2, 3	1, 2, 3, 4
_d_ understand when and how to use fractions and percentages to make proportional comparisons;			4	3, 4	5	3
_e_ understand and use the facilities of a calculator, including the use of the constant function, memory and brackets, to plan a calculation and evaluate expressions;	5, 6	9	4		3, 4	1, 4
_f_ mentally estimate and approximate solutions to numerical calculations, leading to multiplication and division with numbers of any size rounded to one significant figure.	2, 5, 6, 7	1, 2, 9	5		1	2
4 Solving numerical problems Pupils should be taught to:						
_a_ develop an understanding of the four operations and the relationship between them, and apply them to solving problems, including those that involve ratios, proportions and compound measures, using metric or common Imperial units where appropriate;	4, 5, 6, 7, 13, 14, 15	3, 4, 5, 6, 14, 15, 18	4, 5, 9	1, 2, 3, 4	3, 5	1, 3, 4

15

		National Curriculum Levels and *Mathscheck* Tests					
Number (continued)		3	4	5	6	7	8
b	select suitable sequences of operations and methods of computation, including trial-and-improvement methods, to solve problems involving integers, decimals, fractions, ratios and percentages, eg *using a spreadsheet to consider sets of numbers that have a given sum and find the set that has the maximum product;*	5, 6	9	4, 5	1, 2, 3, 4	2, 3, 4	1, 3
c	use a variety of checking strategies and apply them appropriately to calculations; use estimation and inverse operations, and confirm that results are of the right order of magnitude;	2, 4, 6, 7	1, 2, 3, 4, 5, 6, 9, 12	3, 4		1	2
d	give solutions in the context of the problem, selecting an appropriate degree of accuracy, interpreting the display on a calculator, and recognising limitations on the accuracy of data and measurements.	5, 6	9	4	1, 2	3, 4	1, 2

Algebra		3	4	5	6	7	8
1 Pupils should be given opportunities to:							
a	explore a variety of situations that lead to the expression of relationships;	*This section outlines some general aims and required approaches of the Attainment Target.*					
b	consider how relationships between number operations underpin the techniques for manipulating algebraic expressions;						
c	consider how algebra can be used to model real-life situations and solve problems.						
2 Understanding and using functional relationships Pupils should be taught to:							
a	appreciate the use of letters to represent variables;				5, 6, 7	6	4, 5, 6
b	explore number patterns arising from a variety of situations, using computers where appropriate; interpret, generalise and use simple relationships, and generate rules for number sequences; express simple functions initially in words and then symbolically, representing them in graphical or tabular form;	8	11, 12, 13	6	5, 6, 7	6	4, 5, 6
c	interpret graphs that describe real-life situations;	16, 17, 18	20, 21, 22, 23	11, 12, 13		7	8
d	explore the properties of standard mathematical functions, including linear and square, reciprocal and other polynomial functions; make and interpret tables and graphs of functions, sketch their graphs, and use graphical calculators and computers to understand their behaviour.		11	6	7	7	8
3 Understanding and using equations and formulae Pupils should be taught to:							
a	appreciate the use of letters to represent unknowns;				2, 5, 6, 7	6	4, 5, 6
b	construct, interpret and evaluate formulae and expressions, given in words or symbols, related to mathematics or other subjects, or real-life situations, using computers and calculators where appropriate;		11, 12	6	5, 6, 7	6	4, 5
c	manipulate algebraic expressions; form and manipulate equations or inequalities in order to solve problems;				6	7, 8	6

Algebra (continued)

	3	4	5	6	7	8
d solve a range of linear equations, simple linear simultaneous equations, inequalities, and quadratic and higher-order polynomial equations, selecting the most appropriate method for the problem concerned, including trial-and-improvement methods.				2, 6	7, 8	7

Shape, Space and Measures

	3	4	5	6	7	8
1 Pupils should be given opportunities to: *This section outlines some general aims and required approaches of the Attainment Target.*						
a use a variety of different representations;						
b explore shape and space through drawing and practical work using a wide range of materials;						
c use computers to generate and transform graphic images and to solve problems.						
2 Understanding and using properties of shape Pupils should be taught to:						
a visualise, describe and represent shapes, including 2-D representations of 3-D objects, using geometrical language with increasing precision;	9, 10, 11	14, 15	7	8		
b construct 2-D and 3-D shapes from given information; understand the congruence of simple shapes, and classify triangles, quadrilaterals, polygons and other shapes, knowing and using their properties;		14, 15	7	9		
c understand the symmetry properties of 2-D and 3-D shapes and use these to solve problems in two and three dimensions;	12	16, 17	8	10		
d measure angles, and use the language associated with them; explain and use the angle properties of polygons and other 2-D configurations, including those associated with parallel and intersecting lines;	9, 10, 11	15	7	10, 11		
e understand and use Pythagoras' theorem;					9	
f understand the trigonometrical relationships in right-angled triangles, and use these to solve problems, including those involving bearings.						10
3 Understanding and using properties of position, movement and transformation Pupils should be taught to:						
a use co-ordinate systems to specify location, initially using rectangular Cartesian co-ordinates in the first quadrant;		13				
b recognise and visualise the transformations of translation, reflection, rotation and enlargement, and their combination in two dimensions; understand the notations used to describe them;		13, 16, 17	8	12		
c understand and use the properties of transformations to create and analyse patterns, to investigate the properties of shapes, and to derive results, including congruence;	11	13, 16, 17		12		
d develop an understanding of scale, including using and interpreting maps and drawings, and enlarging shapes by different scale factors; develop an understanding of and use mathematical similarity;				15	11	9

Shape, Space and Measures (continued)

	3	4	5	6	7	8
e determine the locus of an object moving according to a given rule, including, where appropriate, using practical methods and the devising of instructions for a computer to produce desired shapes and paths.				12	12	

4 Understanding and using measures
Pupils should be taught to:

	3	4	5	6	7	8
a choose appropriate instruments and standard units of length, mass, capacity and time, and make sensible estimates in everyday situations, extending to less familiar contexts; develop an understanding of the relationship between units, converting one metric unit to another; know Imperial units in daily use and their approximate metric equivalents;	13, 14, 15	14, 15, 18	9, 10			
b develop an understanding of the difference between discrete and continuous measures; read and interpret scales, including decimal scales, and understand the degree of accuracy that is possible, or appropriate, for a given purpose;	13, 14, 15	15	7, 9, 10		13	
c understand and use compound measures, including speed and density;					14	
d find perimeters, areas and volumes of common shapes, including circles and cylinders, by counting and dissection methods, progressing to the derivation and use of standard formulae; distinguish between formulae by considering dimensions, eg *recognise that $\frac{4}{3}\pi r^2$ cannot represent the volume of a sphere.*		19		13, 14	10	11

Handling Data

	3	4	5	6	7	8
1 Pupils should be given opportunities to:						
a formulate questions that can be considered using statistical methods;						
b undertake purposeful enquiries based on data analysis;						
c use computers as a source of large samples, a tool for exploring graphical representations, and as a means to simulate events;		*This section outlines some general aims and required approaches of the Attainment Target.*				
d engage in practical and experimental work in order to appreciate some of the principles which govern random events;						
e look critically at some of the ways in which representations of data can be misleading and conclusions can be uncertain.						

2 Processing and interpreting data – collecting data
Pupils should be taught to:

	3	4	5	6	7	8
a design and use data collection sheets, access required information from tables, lists and computer databases, and make frequency tables for grouped data, where appropriate;	16, 18	20, 22	11, 12	16		
b design a questionnaire or an experiment to capture the data needed to follow lines of enquiry and to test hypotheses, taking possible bias into account;		20	12		15	

Handling Data (continued)

National Curriculum Levels and *Mathscheck* Tests	3	4	5	6	7	8
– representing and analysing data Pupils should be taught to:						
c construct appropriate diagrams and graphs to represent discrete and continuous data, including bar charts, line graphs, pie charts, frequency polygons, scatter diagrams and cumulative frequency diagrams;	17, 18	20, 22, 23		17, 18	17, 18	12
d calculate or estimate, and use appropriate measures of central tendency, ie mode, median and mean, initially with discrete data, progressing to grouped and continuous data;		21, 22	11		16, 17	
e select and calculate or estimate appropriate measures of spread, including the range and interquartile range applied to discrete, grouped and continuous data;		21, 22	11		16, 17	13
– interpreting data Pupils should be taught to:						
f interpret a wide range of graphs and diagrams; draw inferences based on the shapes of graphs and simple statistics for a single distribution, the comparative distribution of sets of data, and the relationships between two sets of data, including correlation and lines of best fit;	16, 17	21, 23	13	17, 19	17, 18	12, 13
g evaluate results critically, and develop an understanding of the reliability of results;			13		16, 17, 18	12, 13
h recognise that inferences drawn from data analysis of an experiment or enquiry may suggest further questions for investigation.					17	13
3 Estimating and calculating the probabilities of events Pupils should be taught to:						
a understand and use the vocabulary of probability, through experience, experiment and theory, leading to understanding and using the probability scale from 0 to 1;		24	14	21	19	
b give and justify estimates of probability to an appropriate degree of accuracy;		24	14			
c understand and use relative frequency as an estimate of probability, and judge when sufficient trials have been carried out;					19	
d recognise situations where probabilities can be based on equally likely outcomes, and others where estimates must be based on experimental evidence, and make these estimates;			15	21	19	
e identify all the outcomes of a combination of two experiments, eg *throwing two dice*; use tabulation, tree diagrams or other diagrammatic representations of compound events;				20		14
f recognise the conditions when the addition of probabilities for mutually exclusive events, and the multiplication of probabilities for two independent events, apply, and make the appropriate calculations.				21		14

Name _____ **Date of birth** _____

	Mathscheck
Attainment Target 1	
Level 3	

Using and Applying Mathematics

		Ma2	Ma3	Ma4
Pupils try different approaches and find ways of overcoming difficulties that arise when they are solving problems	*Tick when attainment has been observed when working in:*			
Can the pupil:				
i	Recognise, and talk about, using mathematics in other subjects?			
ii	Make use of knowledge of other subjects in solving problems?			
iii	Attempt a task with several stages, in a familiar context and with help?			
iv	Choose and use concrete materials to help overcome difficulties in computation and construction?			
v	Use a calculator to help with difficult calculations?			
vi	Plan a suitable sequence of activities to carry out a task, with help?			
vii	Choose and use appropriate equipment to carry out a task?			
viii	Persevere with a task?			
ix	Co-operate with other members of a group?			
x	Carry out one or more defined tasks on behalf of the group?			
[Pupils] are beginning to organise their work and check results				
Can the pupil:				
i	Report verbally on the conduct of a task?			
ii	Present a series of diagrams to record work or results?			
iii	Complete a list, table or chart?			
iv	Interpret a list, table or chart and write about work done?			
v	Make reasonable estimates of possible solutions?			
vi	Use a range of checking devices?			
Pupils discuss their mathematical work and are beginning to explain their thinking				
Can the pupil:				
i	Explain methods of calculation using correct terminology?			
ii	Explain the process or technique being used, using appropriate terminology?			
iii	Sensibly discuss difficulties encountered?			
iv	Show personal control of thoughts and actions, rather than being led by others?			
[Pupils] use and interpret mathematical symbols and diagrams				
Can the pupil:				
i	Use and interpret an appropriate range of mathematical symbols?			
ii	Use and interpret an appropriate range of mathematical diagrams?			
Pupils show that they understand a general statement by finding particular examples that match it				
Can the pupil:				
i	Recognise when the direction of a task is 'going wrong'?			
ii	Recognise when a solution is obviously wrong?			
iii	Link past and present experiences to suggest simple conclusions?			
iv	Suggest appropriate ways to test a predicted solution?			
v	Accept that first attempts do not always work and learn from experience?			

Mathscheck	**Name** _____		**Date of birth** _____	
Attainment Target 1 **Level 4**	**Using and Applying Mathematics**			

		Tick when attainment has been observed when working in:		
Pupils are developing their own strategies for solving problems and are using these strategies both in working within mathematics and in applying mathematics to practical contexts				
Can the pupil:		**Ma2**	**Ma3**	**Ma4**
i	Recall and use a range of materials employed in previous activities?			
ii	Recall and use a range of methods employed in previous activities?			
iii	Personally plan a sequence of activities to carry out a task?			
iv	Take an active part in co-operative group planning of a task?			
v	Use a clearly articulated approach to a task?			
vi	Choose and use materials and resources directly appropriate to a task?			
vii	Attempt to give support to another group member when asked?			
viii	Discuss a range of methods with other group members and the teacher?			
ix	Flexibly follow alternative lines of thought?			
x	Recognise when an investigation has reached a 'dead end'?			
xi	Change to an alternative line of thought without being asked to do so?			
[Pupils] present information and results in a clear and organised way, explaining the reasons for their presentation				
Can the pupil:				
i	Refine the data of a real-world situation into a numerical or geometric form to facilitate calculation or observation of patterns?			
ii	Suggest clear explanations or 'definitions' of mathematical patterns?			
iii	Record work done in: pictorial, written, diagrammatic, graphical, symbolic form?			
iv	Recognise the need for clear and systematic recording to aid understanding and interpretation?			
v	Use various forms of recording as evidence to substantiate verbal explanations?			
[Pupils] search for a pattern by trying out ideas of their own				
Can the pupil:				
i	Recognise and find patterns of numbers, shapes and symbols?			
ii	Recognise and describe relationships between items of information?			
iii	Suggest other possible contexts in which similar solutions might be observed?			
iv	Suggest/predict possible solutions to problems?			
v	Find appropriate examples which confirm or invalidate predictions?			

Mathscheck

Name _____ **Date of birth** _____

Using and Applying Mathematics

	Tick when attainment has been observed when working in:		

In order to carry through tasks and solve mathematical problems, pupils identify and obtain necessary information; they check their results, considering whether these are sensible

Can the pupil:	Ma2	Ma3	Ma4
i Personally plan an effective sequence of activities to carry out a task?			
ii Choose and use a wide range of appropriate mathematical concepts, skills and processes to tackle a task?			
iii Discuss which actions and processes are appropriate (or inappropriate) for a task?			
iv Decide whether available information is relevant or irrelevant to the task?			
v Modify a chosen approach as unforeseen lines of thought emerge?			
vi Review progress with guidance from the teacher?			
vii Work effectively as an active, participating member of groups of various sizes?			
viii Work individually on an extended personal topic in mathematics?			

Pupils show understanding of situations by describing them mathematically using symbols, words and diagrams

Can the pupil:			
i Explain and/or discuss own presentations of information in oral, written, diagrammatic or constructed forms?			
ii Understand and interpret other pupils' presentations of information?			
iii Make sense of media representations of facts, ideas or processes?			
iv Recognise misleading presentations of information?			
v Suggest appropriate ways to improve the clarity of everyday presentations of information?			
vi Operate competently at a personal level in the real world of timetables, schedules and the like?			

[Pupils] make general statements of their own, based on evidence they have produced, and give an explanation of their reasoning

Can the pupil:			
i Systematically follow verbal, written or diagrammatic instructions?			
ii Organise information from the environment in a 'mathematical' way?			
iii Recognise and discuss clues to possible patterns in findings?			
iv Use techniques such as systematic listing to organise numerical data or information?			
v Make 'mathematical' statements to identify the rules or generalisations evident in patterns?			
vi Test the validity of statements by using examples from within the information itself?			

Mathscheck | Name   **Date**

Ma 2, Level 4
Number and algebra
Test 1 Series 1

Place value. Multiplying & dividing by 10 or 100
Level Description element Pupils use their understanding of place value to multiply and divide whole numbers by 10 or 100.

1 Write in **numerals:**

  a seven hundred and five

  b seventeen thousand and seventeen

  c one million

  d one hundred and six thousand and twenty-one

2 Write in **words:**

  a 222

  b 4685

  c 30,035

3 Write these numbers in **descending** order: 12,603 2613 16,302 632 12,360

4 Use only these digits **3 4 7 1 2**. Change the order to make:

  a the largest number   **b** the smallest number

5 Do these in your head. Write the answer only.

  a $5 \times 10 =$ **b** $1 \times 10 =$

  c $10 \times 0 =$ **d** $20 \times 10 =$

  e $50 \times 10 =$ **f** $100 \times 10 =$

  g $10 \times 10 =$ **h** $0 \times 100 =$

6 Do these in your head. Write the answer only.

  a $90 \div 10 =$ **b** $10 \div 10 =$

  c $600 \div 10 =$ **d** $700 \div 100 =$

  e $40 \times$ ( ) $= 400$ **f** ( ) $\times 7 = 700$

  g $1000 \div 10 =$ **h** $5000 \div 100 =$

Mathscheck | **Name** | **Date**

Ma 2, Level 4
Number and algebra
Test 1 Series 1

Place value. Multiplying & dividing by 10 or 100

Level Description element Pupils use their understanding of place value to multiply and
divide whole numbers by 10 or 100.

7 What is the value of the 4 in these numbers?

   a   243 → 4 ( )

   b   4567 → 4 ( )

   c   4,111,222 → 4 ( )

   d   234,211 → 4 ( )

8 Write the number which is:

   a   10 more than 595

   b   100 more than 757

   c   1 more than 2000

   d   1000 more than 24,132

9 Write the number which is:

   a   1 less than 700

   b   10 less than 2000

   c   100 less than 1562

   d   1000 less than 1624

10

   a   3000 = ( ) hundreds

   b   2500 = ( ) tens

   c   132,400 = ( ) hundreds

   d   2 million = ( ) thousands

11 Write the answer only.

   a   10 × 18 = ( )

   b   100 × 36 = ( )

12 Write the answer only.

   a   10 × 254 = ( )

   b   100 × 555 = ( )

13 A computer disk costs 90p, so:

   a   10 disks cost ( )

   b   100 disks cost ( )

14 A box of 100 postcards costs £12, so:

   a   1 postcard costs ( )

   b   1000 postcards cost ( )

Mathscheck

Name   **Date**

Ma 2, Level 4

Number and algebra

Test 2 Series 1

Mental recall of multiplication facts to 10 × 10

Level Description element In solving number problems, pupils use a range of mental and written methods of computation with the four operations, including mental recall of

1 Do these in your head. Write the answers only.

4 × 4 =	6 × 6 =	9 × 7 =
3 × 7 =	8 × 4 =	7 × 9 =
8 × 7 =	3 × 6 =	4 × 3 =
7 × 3 =	3 × 3 =	3 × 5 =
5 × 5 =	9 × 6 =	4 × 9 =
9 × 5 =	9 × 3 =	9 × 4 =
9 × 9 =	7 × 2 =	8 × 6 =
6 × 7 =	1 × 8 =	7 × 7 =
5 × 8 =	4 × 10 =	5 × 4 =
4 × 8 =	4 × 6 =	5 × 6 =
8 × 3 =	8 × 9 =	3 × 8 =
7 × 5 =	7 × 6 =	7 × 4 =
6 × 9 =	5 × 9 =	8 × 8 =
7 × 8 =	6 × 3 =	3 × 9 =
5 × 3 =	3 × 4 =	6 × 8 =
9 × 8 =	3 × 2 =	6 × 5 =
2 × 7 =	5 × 7 =	4 × 7 =
6 × 4 =	8 × 5 =	4 × 5 =

Name   **Date**

Adding numbers with up to three digits

Level Description element In solving number problems, pupils use a range of mental and written methods of computation with the four operations, including mental recall of multiplication facts up to 10×10.

1 a
$$\begin{array}{r} 36 \\ +\ \ 3 \\ \hline \end{array}$$

b
$$\begin{array}{r} 58 \\ +\ \ 8 \\ \hline \end{array}$$

c
$$\begin{array}{r} 26 \\ +\ 17 \\ \hline \end{array}$$

2 a
$$\begin{array}{r} 58 \\ +\ 65 \\ \hline \end{array}$$

b
$$\begin{array}{r} 284 \\ +\ \ \ 5 \\ \hline \end{array}$$

c
$$\begin{array}{r} 348 \\ +\ \ \ 6 \\ \hline \end{array}$$

3 a
$$\begin{array}{r} 324 \\ +\ \ 33 \\ \hline \end{array}$$

b
$$\begin{array}{r} 729 \\ +\ \ 28 \\ \hline \end{array}$$

c
$$\begin{array}{r} 283 \\ +\ \ 42 \\ \hline \end{array}$$

4 a
$$\begin{array}{r} 397 \\ +\ \ 56 \\ \hline \end{array}$$

b
$$\begin{array}{r} 241 \\ +\ 126 \\ \hline \end{array}$$

c
$$\begin{array}{r} 328 \\ +\ 646 \\ \hline \end{array}$$

5 a
$$\begin{array}{r} 573 \\ +\ 174 \\ \hline \end{array}$$

b
$$\begin{array}{r} 485 \\ +\ 196 \\ \hline \end{array}$$

c
$$\begin{array}{r} 777 \\ +\ 666 \\ \hline \end{array}$$

Name   *Date*

Subtracting numbers with up to three digits

Level Description element In solving number problems, pupils use a range of mental and written methods of computation with the four operations, including mental recall of multiplication facts up to 10×10.

1 a
$$\begin{array}{r} 67 \\ -\ 34 \\ \hline \end{array}$$

b
$$\begin{array}{r} 82 \\ -\ 27 \\ \hline \end{array}$$

2 a
$$\begin{array}{r} 459 \\ -\ 27 \\ \hline \end{array}$$

b
$$\begin{array}{r} 678 \\ -\ 263 \\ \hline \end{array}$$

3 a
$$\begin{array}{r} 555 \\ -\ 8 \\ \hline \end{array}$$

b
$$\begin{array}{r} 384 \\ -\ 59 \\ \hline \end{array}$$

4 a
$$\begin{array}{r} 573 \\ -\ 228 \\ \hline \end{array}$$

b
$$\begin{array}{r} 472 \\ -\ 91 \\ \hline \end{array}$$

5 a
$$\begin{array}{r} 368 \\ -\ 183 \\ \hline \end{array}$$

b
$$\begin{array}{r} 523 \\ -\ 278 \\ \hline \end{array}$$

6 a
$$\begin{array}{r} 620 \\ -\ 187 \\ \hline \end{array}$$

b
$$\begin{array}{r} 702 \\ -\ 384 \\ \hline \end{array}$$

Name   **Date**

Multiplying numbers up to 100 by single-digit numbers

Level Description element In solving number problems, pupils use a range of mental and written methods of computation with the four operations, including mental recall of multiplication facts up to 10×10.

1 a
$$\begin{array}{r} 13 \\ \times\ \ 3 \\ \hline \end{array}$$

b
$$\begin{array}{r} 14 \\ \times\ \ 5 \\ \hline \end{array}$$

2 a
$$\begin{array}{r} 27 \\ \times\ \ 3 \\ \hline \end{array}$$

b
$$\begin{array}{r} 34 \\ \times\ \ 3 \\ \hline \end{array}$$

3 a
$$\begin{array}{r} 15 \\ \times\ \ 7 \\ \hline \end{array}$$

b
$$\begin{array}{r} 46 \\ \times\ \ 7 \\ \hline \end{array}$$

4 a
$$\begin{array}{r} 55 \\ \times\ \ 6 \\ \hline \end{array}$$

b
$$\begin{array}{r} 68 \\ \times\ \ 7 \\ \hline \end{array}$$

5 a
$$\begin{array}{r} 74 \\ \times\ \ 5 \\ \hline \end{array}$$

b
$$\begin{array}{r} 88 \\ \times\ \ 8 \\ \hline \end{array}$$

Name   **Date**

Dividing numbers up to 100 by single-digit numbers

Level Description element In solving number problems, pupils use a range of mental and written methods of computation with the four operations, including mental recall of multiplication facts up to 10×10.

Work out the answers to these 'division' calculations. Show the working.

1	$72 \div 9$	
	Answer	
2	$63 \div 7$	
	Answer	

3	$60 \div 2$	
	Answer	
4	$60 \div 3$	
	Answer	

5	$84 \div 2$	
	Answer	
6	$69 \div 3$	
	Answer	

7	$48 \div 3$	
	Answer	
8	$91 \div 7$	
	Answer	

9	$83 \div 6$	
	Answer	
10	$67 \div 5$	
	Answer	

Name   **Date**

Adding decimals to two places
Level Description element [Pupils] add and subtract decimals to two places.

1 a
$$4 \cdot 2$$
$$+\ 0 \cdot 7$$

b
$$4 \cdot 6$$
$$+\ 0 \cdot 5$$

c
$$2 \cdot 5$$
$$+\ 1 \cdot 8$$

2 a
$$3 \cdot 5$$
$$+\ 9 \cdot 6$$

b
$$2 \cdot 63$$
$$+\ 0 \cdot 06$$

c
$$5 \cdot 17$$
$$+\ 0 \cdot 08$$

3 a
$$2 \cdot 61$$
$$+\ 0 \cdot 27$$

b
$$6 \cdot 54$$
$$+\ 0 \cdot 36$$

c
$$1 \cdot 75$$
$$+\ 0 \cdot 62$$

4 a
$$4 \cdot 79$$
$$+\ 0 \cdot 65$$

b
$$4 \cdot 27$$
$$+\ 2 \cdot 32$$

c
$$3 \cdot 46$$
$$+\ 6 \cdot 28$$

5 a
$$5 \cdot 65$$
$$+\ 2 \cdot 83$$

b
$$3 \cdot 96$$
$$+\ 2 \cdot 85$$

c
$$5 \cdot 88$$
$$+\ 6 \cdot 25$$

Mathscheck	**Name**		**Date**
Ma 2, Level 4	**Subtracting decimals to two places**		
Number and algebra	Level Description element [Pupils] add and subtract decimals to two places.		
Test 8 Series 1			

1 a
$$\begin{array}{r} 5 \cdot 8 \\ - 2 \cdot 6 \\ \hline \end{array}$$
b
$$\begin{array}{r} 7 \cdot 3 \\ - 3 \cdot 6 \\ \hline \end{array}$$

2 a
$$\begin{array}{r} 3 \cdot 95 \\ - 0 \cdot 72 \\ \hline \end{array}$$
b
$$\begin{array}{r} 5 \cdot 92 \\ - 2 \cdot 31 \\ \hline \end{array}$$

3 a
$$\begin{array}{r} 4 \cdot 44 \\ - 0 \cdot 07 \\ \hline \end{array}$$
b
$$\begin{array}{r} 2 \cdot 72 \\ - 0 \cdot 46 \\ \hline \end{array}$$

4 a
$$\begin{array}{r} 6 \cdot 91 \\ - 4 \cdot 79 \\ \hline \end{array}$$
b
$$\begin{array}{r} 5 \cdot 58 \\ - 0 \cdot 64 \\ \hline \end{array}$$

5 a
$$\begin{array}{r} 4 \cdot 47 \\ - 2 \cdot 62 \\ \hline \end{array}$$
b
$$\begin{array}{r} 6 \cdot 15 \\ - 2 \cdot 89 \\ \hline \end{array}$$

6 a
$$\begin{array}{r} 7 \cdot 60 \\ - 3 \cdot 78 \\ \hline \end{array}$$
b
$$\begin{array}{r} 6 \cdot 07 \\ - 1 \cdot 28 \\ \hline \end{array}$$

Ma 2, Level 4

Number and algebra

Test 9 Series 1

Rounding & approximating. Interpreting calculator displays

Level Description element In solving problems with or without a calculator, pupils check the reasonableness of their results by reference to their knowledge of the context or to the size of the numbers.

---

1 Round these numbers to the nearest 10.

    a   57

    b   265

    c   15,484

2 Round these numbers to the nearest 100.

    a   629

    b   1250

    c   26,257

---

3 Round these numbers to the nearest 1000.

    a   1587

    b   17,246

    c   121,712

4 Round these numbers to the nearest whole number.

    a   6·4

    b   95·6

    c   1254·5

---

5 Choose and ring the 'best guess' of the answer to these calculations.

a	236 + 381	550	600	620	650
b	2643 + 1989	4400	4500	4600	4700
c	621 – 187	370	400	430	460
d	2500 – 1678	600	700	800	900

---

6 A pad of 100 sheets of paper is 1·5 cm thick.

      Use a calculator

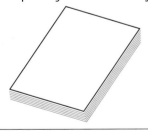

    a   1 sheet has a thickness of (   ) mm

    b   280 sheets have a thickness of (   ) cm

---

7 Write the missing numbers in these 'chains'.

      Use a calculator

    a   [4] (+ 3·3) = ( ) (×) = 14·6 (– 5·9) [ ] =

    b   [7·7] (÷) = 1·1 (+ 7·9) = ( ) (÷ 3) [ ] =

    c   [0·6] (÷) = 0·2 (+ 9·8) = ( ) (÷) [ ] = 2·5

Ma 2, Level 4

Number and algebra

Test 9 Series 1

Rounding & approximating. Interpreting calculator displays

Level Description element In solving problems with or without a calculator, pupils check the reasonableness of their results by reference to their knowledge of the context or to the size of the numbers.

---

8 Round each of the calculator displays to the **nearest whole number.**

a $\boxed{3.14876}$ $\longrightarrow$ ◯

b $\boxed{1.9090909}$ $\longrightarrow$ ◯

c $\boxed{7.08088}$ $\longrightarrow$ ◯

d $\boxed{0.77777}$ $\longrightarrow$ ◯

---

9 Use a calculator. Write the calculator answer **and** round it to the **nearest whole number**.

calculator   to the nearest whole number

a $16\cdot27 + 29\cdot84$

b $72\cdot35 - 37\cdot68$

c $8 \times 0\cdot91$

d $87\cdot6 \div 4$

---

10 A family gets 7 newspapers each week, each costing 42p. The bill comes every 4 weeks. What is the total bill to the **nearest** £1?

£ ☐

---

11 What length of wood is left if four pieces measuring 1 m 34 cm, 92 cm, 1 m 87 cm and 3 m are cut from a plank 10 metres long? (Answer in metres.)

☐ m

12 Wire netting is sold **only** in full 1 metre lengths. How many metres must I buy to enclose this rectangular rabbit run?

1m 20 cm

88 cm  88 cm

1m 20 cm

☐ m

Fractions & percentages to describe proportions

Level Description element [Pupils] recognise approximate proportions of a whole and use simple fractions and percentages to describe these.

---

1 Shade $\frac{3}{5}$.

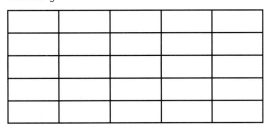

2 Shade $\frac{5}{8}$.

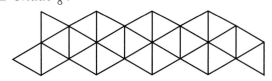

3
Mark and label these points on the road from A to B.

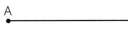

Q is about $\frac{3}{4}$ of the distance from A to B.

R is about $\frac{1}{3}$ of the distance from A to B.

S is about $\frac{2}{3}$ of the distance from A to B.

4
Mark and label these points on the road from A to B.

A ●————————————————● B

D is about $\frac{1}{10}$ of the distance from A to B.

E is about $\frac{2}{5}$ of the distance from A to B.

F is about $\frac{7}{10}$ of the distance from A to B.

---

5 Shade 0·46 of this square.

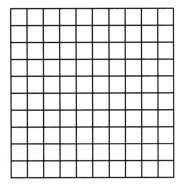

6 Shade 27% of this square.

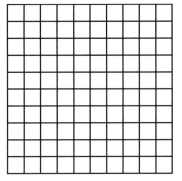

---

7 What percentage of the circle is:

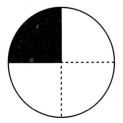

a black ⬭ %

b white ⬭ %

8 In a box of 30 pencils 15 are broken. What **percentage** are broken?

⬭ %

9 In a class of 25 children, 12 are girls. What **percentage** are **boys?**

⬭ %

Ma 2, Level 4
Number and algebra
Test 11 Series 1

Number patterns & related terminology

Level Description element Pupils explore and describe number patterns, and relationships including multiple, factor and square.

1 In this set of numbers a line of four has been ringed.

Explain why they make a number pattern.

_____

_____

_____

_____

_____

2	3	4	5	6
12	13	14	15	16
22	23	24	25	26
32	33	34	35	36
42	43	44	45	46

2 Look carefully at this set of numbers.

Ring four numbers in a line which make a pattern.

Explain why they make a number pattern.

_____

_____

_____

_____

2	6	10	14	18
4	12	20	28	36
6	18	30	42	54
8	24	40	56	72
10	30	50	70	90

Number patterns & related terminology

Level Description element Pupils explore and describe number patterns, and relationships including multiple, factor and square.

3 Look at these patterns of matchsticks.

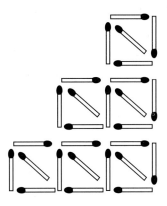

5 matchsticks

9 matchsticks

13 matchsticks

a Draw the next pattern.

b Write the next number.

c Write sentences about the patterns of shapes and numbers.

_____

_____

_____

_____

4 Complete these 'doubling and halving' patterns.

a $1 \times 72 = 2 \times \boxed{} = \boxed{} \times 18 = 8 \times \boxed{}$

b $3 \times 32 = 6 \times \boxed{} = \boxed{} \times 8 = 24 \times \boxed{}$

5 If $13 \times 23 = 299$ which three of these number statements are true? (Tick your choices.)

a $23 + 13 = 299$

b $299 \div 13 = 23$

c $299 \div 23 = 13$

d $299 - 23 = 13$

e $23 \times 13 = 299$

Name   **Date**

Number patterns & related terminology

Level Description element Pupils explore and describe number patterns, and relationships including multiple, factor and square.

Write the missing numbers.

6

2,   4,   6,   8,   ( ) , ( )

7

3,   6,   9, ( ) , ( ) , 18

8

25,   20,   15, ( ) , ( ) , 0

9

596,   597,   598, ( ) , ( )

10

40,   37,   34, ( ) , ( )

11

160,   80,   40, ( ) , ( )

12

1,   2,   4,   8,   16, ( ) , ( )

13

1,   3,   6,   10 , ( ) , ( )

14 Look at these numbers.

27   45   80   28
10   30   6

Write those which are:

a multiples of 2   ◯ ◯ ◯ ◯ ◯

b multiples of 10   ◯ ◯ ◯

c multiples of 5   ◯ ◯ ◯ ◯

d multiples of 2 **and** 5   ◯ ◯ ◯

e multiples of 2 **and** 10   ◯ ◯ ◯

15 Complete this statement:

The **factors** of 24 are [   ]

Name   **Date**

Using simple formulae expressed in words

Level Description element [Pupils] have begun to use simple formulae expressed in words.

1 Write the missing numbers.

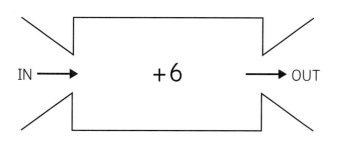

IN	OUT
4	
9	
	14
	19

2 Write the missing numbers.

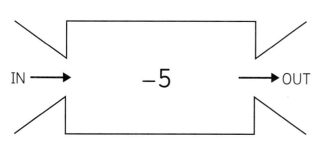

IN	OUT
12	
20	
	11
	20

3 Write the missing numbers.

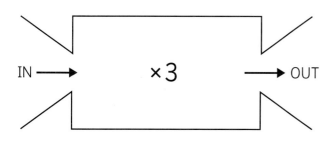

IN	OUT
4	
10	
	15
	21

4 Write the missing numbers.

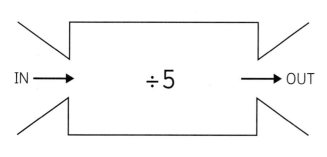

IN	OUT
30	
50	
	8
	7

Using simple formulae expressed in words
Level Description element [Pupils] have begun to use simple formulae expressed in words.

5 Write the missing numbers in the OUT column.

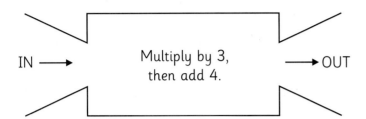

IN	OUT
3	
5	
8	

6 Write the missing numbers in the IN column.

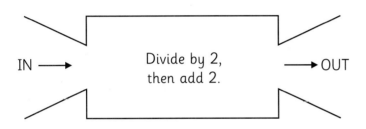

IN	OUT
	20
	12
	8

7 Write the missing numbers.

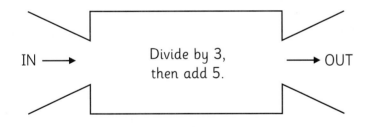

IN	OUT
15	
	12
30	

8 Look at these numbers.   Write the rule which changes the IN numbers to OUT numbers.

IN	OUT
1	8
4	14
6	18

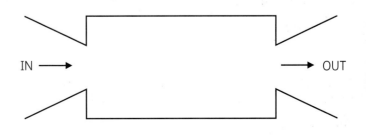

Using simple formulae expressed in words

Level Description element [Pupils] have begun to use simple formulae expressed in words.

9 I add 5 to a number, then multiply the result by 2. The answer is 16.
What number did I start with?

I started with ⬭

10 I double a number, then add 3 and the result is 29.
What is the number I started with?

I started with ⬭

11 Write the missing number.

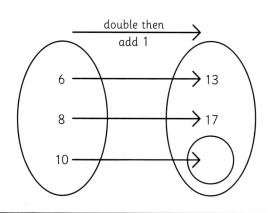

double then add 1

6 → 13
8 → 17
10 → ◯

12 Write the missing number.

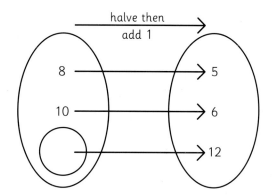

halve then add 1

8 → 5
10 → 6
◯ → 12

13 Complete the rule.

Week	1	2	3	4	5	6				
Total pocket money	£1	£2	£3	£4	£5	£6				

Rule:

Total pocket money = (£ ⬭) × number of ⬭

14 Complete the rule.

Jane's age	6	7	8	9	10	11				
Karim's age	1	2	3	4	5	6				

Rule:

Jane's age = ⬭ 's age + ⬭

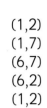

Mathscheck

Ma 2, Level 4

Number and algebra

Test 13 Series 1

Name   **Date**

Using & interpreting co-ordinates in the first quadrant

Level Description element Pupils use and interpret co-ordinates in the first quadrant.

1 Plot these co-ordinates, then join them in the same order to draw a shape.

a

(1,2)
(1,7)
(6,7)
(6,2)
(1,2)

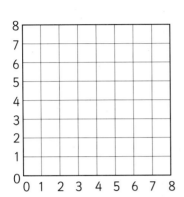

b

(2,2)
(0,6)
(5,6)
(7,2)
(2,2)

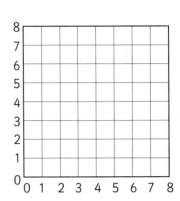

c

(4,7)
(7,5)
(7,3)
(4,1)
(1,3)
(1,5)
(4,7)

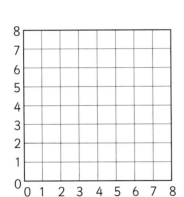

d

(6,8)
(2,8)
(0,6)
(0,3)
(2,1)
(6,1)
(8,3)
(8,6)
(6,8)

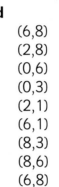

e

(3,6)
(2,2)
(7,2)
(6,6)
(3,6)

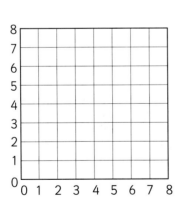

f

(1,7)
(3,1)
(5,7)
(3,4)
(1,7)

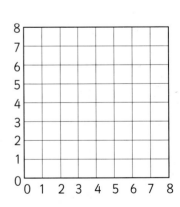

g

(7,0)
(4,7)
(1,6)
(0,3)
(7,0)

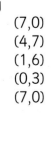

h

(1,4)
(4,7)
(7,4)
(4,1)
(1,4)

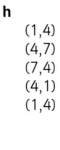

Ma 3, Level 4

Shape, space
and measures

Test 14 Series 1

Constructing simple 3-D models from nets

Level Description element Pupils make 3-D mathematical models by linking given faces or edges, draw common 2-D shapes in different orientations on grids, and identify congruent shapes and orders of rotational symmetry.

1 Use centimetre squared paper, scissors, ruler, pencil and glue.
  a On the squared paper, draw the **nets** to make each shape.
  b Construct the 3-D shape from the net, full size.

Look carefully at the measurements!

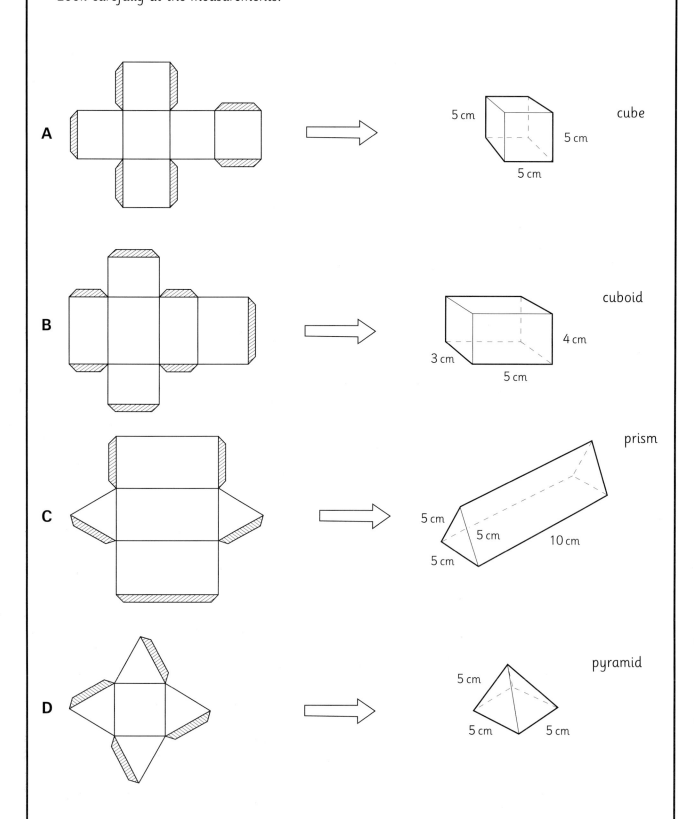

A   cube
    5 cm   5 cm
                5 cm

B   cuboid
                4 cm
    3 cm
    5 cm

C   prism
    5 cm
    5 cm   10 cm
    5 cm

D   pyramid
    5 cm
    5 cm   5 cm

Name **Date**

Ma 3, Level 4

Shape, space and measures

Test 15 Series 1

Constructing 2-D shapes & identifying congruence

Level Description element Pupils make 3-D mathematical models by linking given faces or edges, draw common 2-D shapes in different orientations on grids, and identify congruent shapes and orders of rotational symmetry.

You need: compasses, ruler, sharp pencil, set square.

1 Join the angle to the correct name.

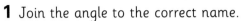

(acute angle)   (right angle)   (reflex angle)   (obtuse angle)

2 Draw a line which is **parallel** to the line AB.

3 Draw a **diagonal** on this shape.

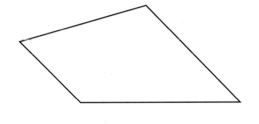

4 Draw a line from P, which is **perpendicular** to the line XY.

5 a Draw a **square** of side 4·5 cm.

 b Mark its **centre** with a clear 'dot' and label it C.

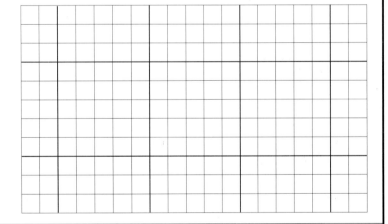

6 a Draw a **rectangle** measuring $8\frac{1}{2}$ cm by $3\frac{1}{2}$ cm.

 b Mark its **centre** with a clear 'dot' and label it C.

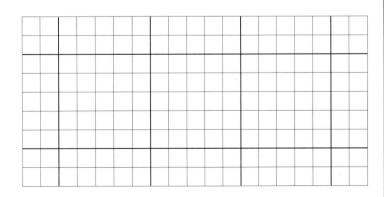

Ma 3, Level 4

Shape, space and measures

Test 15 Series 1

Constructing 2-D shapes & identifying congruence

Level Description element Pupils make 3-D mathematical models by linking given faces or edges, draw common 2-D shapes in different orientations on grids, and identify congruent shapes and orders of rotational symmetry.

---

7 a Draw a circle of radius 2·5 cm.
  b Draw a diameter on it.

8 Use a pair of compasses, a ruler and a pencil.
Bisect this angle.

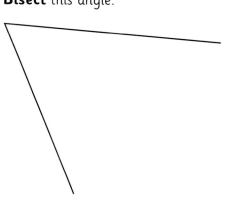

---

9 Use a pair of compasses, a ruler and a pencil.
Draw this triangle full size.

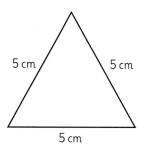

5 cm   5 cm

5 cm

---

10 Use a pair of compasses, a ruler and a pencil.
Draw this triangle full size.

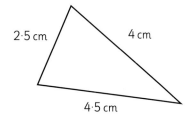

2·5 cm   4 cm

4·5 cm

---

11 Join pairs of **congruent** shapes.

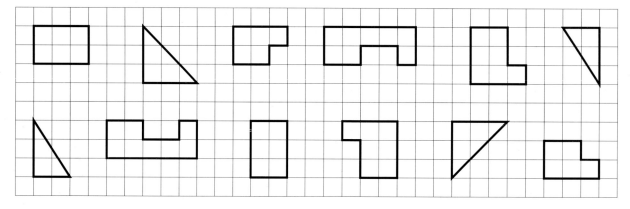

Ma 3, Level 4

Shape, space
and measures

Test 16 Series 1

Identifying orders of rotational symmetry

Level Description element Pupils make 3-D mathematical models by linking given faces or edges, draw common 2-D shapes in different orientations on grids, and identify congruent shapes and orders of rotational symmetry.

1 Write on each shape its order of rotational symmetry.

Use tracing paper to help you to decide.

a

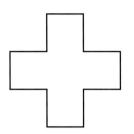

b

c

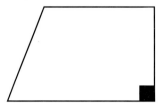

d

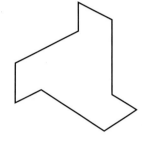

e

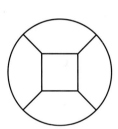

f

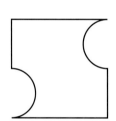

g

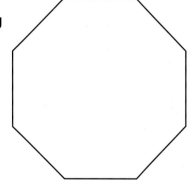

2 This is $\frac{1}{4}$ of a shape. Use tracing paper to help you finish it to make a shape with rotational symmetry of order 4.

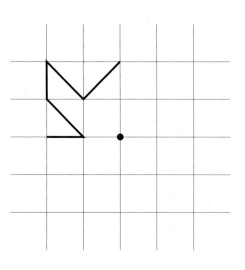

3 Ring the letters which have rotational symmetry of order 2 or more.

Name   **Date**

Reflecting simple shapes in a mirror line

Level Description element [Pupils] reflect simple shapes in a mirror line.

1 Reflect the designs in the mirror lines to show 2-D symmetrical shapes.

Mathscheck

Name   **Date**

Ma 3, Level 4

Shape, space
and measures

Test 18 Series 1

Interpreting numbers on measuring instruments

Level Description element [Pupils] choose and use appropriate units and instruments, interpreting, with appropriate accuracy, numbers on a range of measuring instruments.

1 This scale represents a distance of 2 metres.

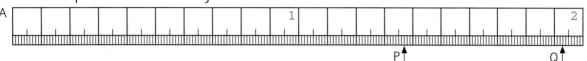

Write in **decimal form** the measurement from A shown by the arrows.

P is (   ) metres from A.   Q is (   ) metres from A.

2 Write the times shown in digital form.

a

(   )

b

(   )

3 Write the weights shown on the scales.

a

(   )

b

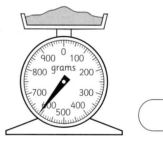

(   )

4 Write the the amount of liquid in each container.

a

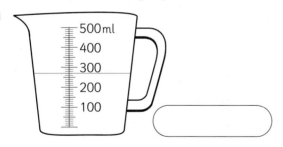

(   )

b

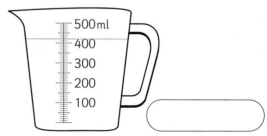

(   )

5 Write the size of these angles.

a

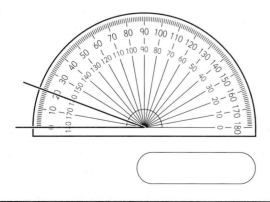

(   )

b

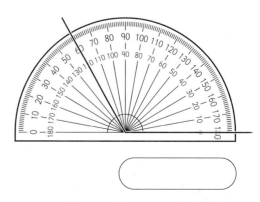

(   )

Finding perimeters, areas & volumes by counting

Level Description element [Pupils] find perimeters of simple shapes, find areas by counting squares, and find volumes by counting cubes.

---

1 What is the **perimeter** of each shape?

Hint: they are drawn on 1 cm grids.

a   **b**   **c**

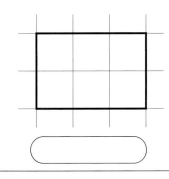 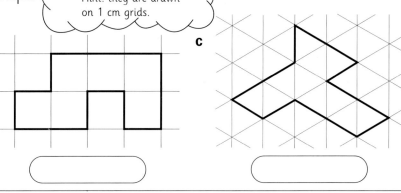

---

2 Calculate the **perimeter** of each shape. (Not drawn to scale.)

a

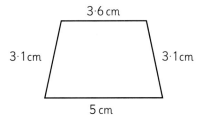

3·6 cm

3·1 cm   3·1 cm

5 cm

perimeter is ⬭ cm

b

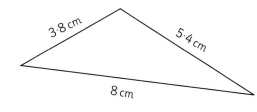

3·8 cm   5·4 cm

8 cm

perimeter is ⬭ cm

---

3 Draw a shape with a **perimeter** of 18 cm.

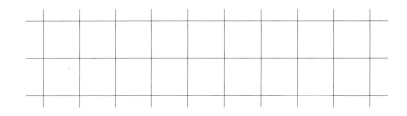

---

4 Write the **area** of each shape (in cm²).

a

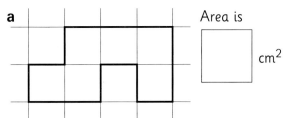

Area is ☐ cm²

b

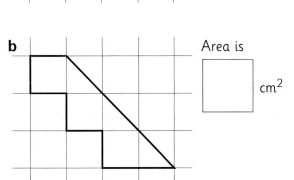

Area is ☐ cm²

5 Write the **area** of each shape (in cm²).

a

Area is ☐ cm²

b

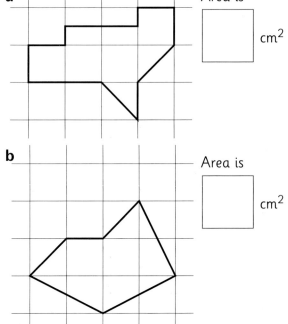

Area is ☐ cm²

Mathscheck

Ma 3, Level 4

Shape, space and measures

Test 19 Series 1

Name

Date

Finding perimeters, areas & volumes by counting

Level Description element [Pupils] find perimeters of simple shapes, find areas by counting squares, and find volumes by counting cubes.

6 Find the approximate **area** of this shape (in cm²).

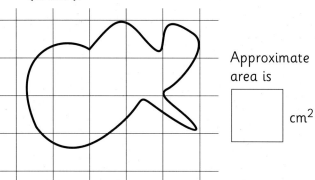

Approximate area is

☐ cm²

7 Draw a shape with an **area** of $7\frac{1}{2}$ cm².

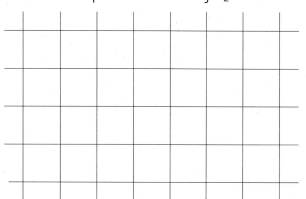

8 These shapes are made using centimetre cubes. Count the cubes to find the **volume** of each shape.

Note that some cubes are hidden behind others.

a

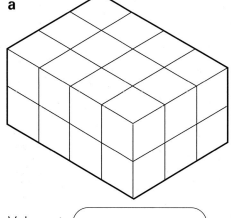

Volume is ⬭ cm³

b

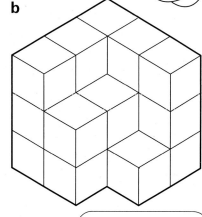

Volume is ⬭ cm³

9 These shapes use centimetre cubes, and some have been cut in half. Find the **volume** of each shape.

a

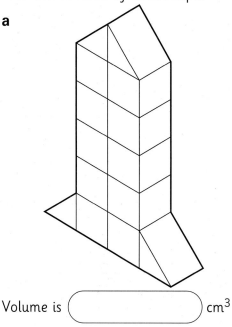

Volume is ⬭ cm³

b

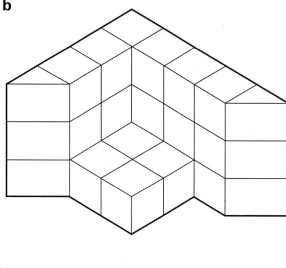

Volume is ⬭ cm³

Name   ***Date***

Collecting & recording data

Level Description element Pupils collect discrete data and record them using a frequency table.

1 Choose a topic for which data would have to be collected. Write its title here.

2 Use this grid to help you draw a tally chart or frequency table. Use your chart or table to record your data.

3 Draw a chart or graph of your data on this grid.

Name   **Date**

Recognising & using the mode & median

Level Description element [Pupils] understand and use the mode and median.

1 Write the **mode** of each set of numbers.

a 8   7   7   8   7   6   7   Mode is (   )

b 7   3   7   5   7   4   3   7   7   3   Mode is (   )

c 8·5   9·2   8·5   9·2   8·5   Mode is (   )
    9·1   9·2   8·5

2 Write the **median** of each set of numbers.

a 4   3   4   3   5   Median is (   )

b 9   9   10   10   10   10   11   Median is (   )

c 1·36   1·29   1·51   1·34   1·25   Median is (   )
    1·40   1·31

3 This table shows the shoe sizes of 30 children in a class.

Kamaljit	$4\frac{1}{2}$	Paul	4	Hayley	6
Laura	1	Tony	$3\frac{1}{2}$	Harpreet	$6\frac{1}{2}$
Monica	$3\frac{1}{2}$	Charlotte	3	Nichola	$4\frac{1}{2}$
Alex	2	Imran	4	Sandeep	$4\frac{1}{2}$
Bhuddi	$4\frac{1}{2}$	Cherie	3	Nusrat	$1\frac{1}{2}$
Nina	5	Morag	$5\frac{1}{2}$	Scott	7
Ian	$4\frac{1}{2}$	Jaimeet	5	Khurram	$4\frac{1}{2}$
Chris	$5\frac{1}{2}$	Diego	$3\frac{1}{2}$	Mike	$6\frac{1}{2}$
Kate	$4\frac{1}{2}$	Pritam	4	Mira	2
Alan	5	Nasreen	4	Karen	$2\frac{1}{2}$

a Complete this table of the shoe sizes.

Shoe size	1	$1\frac{1}{2}$	2	$2\frac{1}{2}$	3	$3\frac{1}{2}$	4	$4\frac{1}{2}$	5	$5\frac{1}{2}$	6	$6\frac{1}{2}$	7
Number of children													

b The median shoe size is (   )

c The modal shoe size is (   )

Ma 4, Level 4

Handling data

Test 22 Series 1

Representing & interpreting data in equal class intervals

Level Description element [Pupils] group data, where appropriate, in equal class intervals, represent collected data in frequency diagrams and interpret such diagrams.

1 Tariq made a list of the number of items in the desk or locker of each of his friends.

10	8	11	16	11	15	12	11	9	10	11	12	11
9	8	17	12	15	12	17	8	12	17	16	17	14
14	13	12	10	10	8	8	10	12	16	12	9	10

a Complete this tally chart of the data.

Number of items	Tally	Frequency
8 – 9		
10 – 11		
12 – 13		
14 – 15		
16 – 17		

b Draw a frequency diagram of the results on this grid.

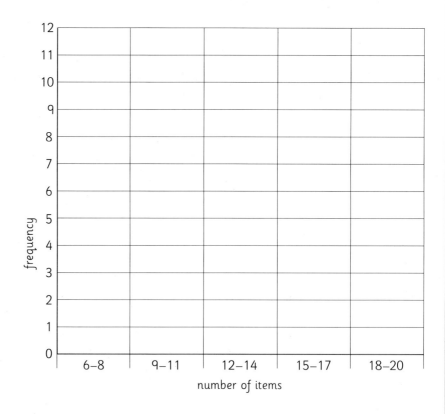

c Complete these statements about the data.

The median is ⬭   The mode is ⬭

Ma 4, Level 4	**Constructing & interpreting simple line graphs**
Handling data	Level Description element [Pupils] construct and interpret simple line graphs.
Test 23 Series 1	

1 Draw a bar-line graph of this data.

Score when rolling a dice 120 times	
Score	Frequency (Number of times)
1	15
2	24
3	20
4	18
5	22
6	21

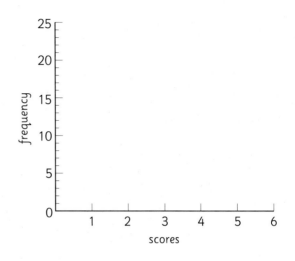

2 Answer the questions about this line graph of temperatures.

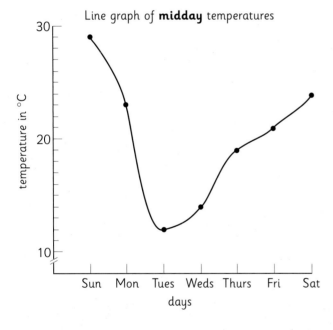

Line graph of **midday** temperatures

a What was the highest temperature recorded? ◯ °C

b What was the lowest temperature recorded? ◯ °C

c What was the range of temperatures recorded? ◯ °C

d What does the graph show as the approximate temperature at **midnight** between Wednesday and Thursday? ◯ °C

e Write why this is only a guess at the temperature at midnight.

Probability: certainty & uncertainty, likelihood & fairness

Level Description element [Pupils] understand and use simple vocabulary associated with probability, including 'fair', 'certain' and 'likely'.

Tick the correct word.

1 The day after Friday will be Saturday:

certain
uncertain
impossible

2 It will rain on your birthday:

certain
uncertain
impossible

3 The first cube you take from the box will be red:

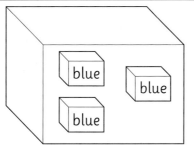

certain
uncertain
impossible

4 You will see a green bike today:

certain
uncertain
impossible

5 If you roll a die it will score 2:

certain
uncertain
impossible

6 A spider will say your name today:

certain
uncertain
impossible

7 Are these events **more likely** or **less likely** to happen?
Write 'more' or 'less' in the correct spaces.

likely   likely   likely   likely

8 A packet of sweets has these numbers of different colours.

Colour	Number
red	15
yellow	2
brown	10
pink	7

I tip out one sweet.
a Which colour am I **most likely** to tip out?
b Write why you chose that colour.

c Which colour am I **least likely** to tip out?

9 Are these events   **very likely** ,   **likely** ,   **unlikely**   or   **very unlikely**   to happen?

a You will be in Australia tomorrow.

b It will be icy next winter.

c There will be a cartoon on television at 5 o'clock.

d Someone in your class will have a birthday next month.

Mathscheck	**Name**		**Date**
Ma 4, Level 4	**Probability: certainty & uncertainty, likelihood & fairness**		
Handling data Test 24 Series 1	**Level Description element** [Pupils] understand and use simple vocabulary associated with probability, including 'fair', 'certain' and 'likely'.		

10 Look at this spinner.

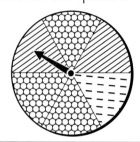

After spinning the pointer:
a the **most likely** result is

b the **least likely** result is

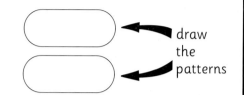

draw the patterns

11 Colour these spinners so that the result of a spin:

a   is **likely** to point to blue   **b**   is **certain** to point to red   **c**   has **no chance** of pointing to blue

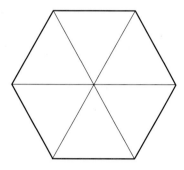   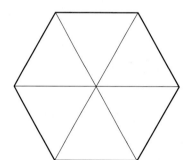   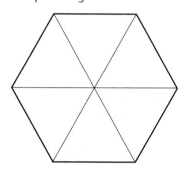

d   is **unlikely** to point to yellow   **e**   has an **even chance** of pointing to the red or green   **f**   is **equally likely** to score red, blue or yellow

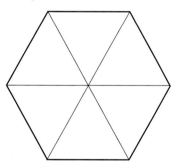   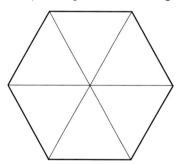   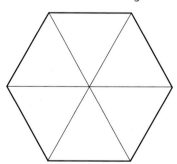

12 Are these dice games **fair** or **unfair**?

a James has to roll 1 or 2 to win. Janet has to roll 5 or 6 to win.

b Mary has to roll an even number to win. Freddie has to roll 1 or 6 to win.

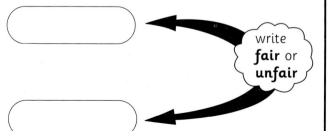

write **fair** or **unfair**

Ma 2, Level 4

Number and algebra

Test 1 Series 2

Place value. Multiplying & dividing by 10 or 100

Level Description element Pupils use their understanding of place value to multiply and divide whole numbers by 10 or 100.

1 Write in **numerals:**

  a   six hundred and eight

  b   sixteen thousand and four

  c   three million

  d   two hundred and four thousand and five

2 Write in **words:**

  a   409

  b   2929

  c   61,030

3 Write these numbers in **ascending** order: 3412   40,123   12,340   1430   23,140

4 Use only these digits   **5   7   1   1   3**. Change the order to make:

  a   the smallest number   **b**   the largest number

5 Do these in your head. Write the answer only.

  a $10 \times 1 =$ **b** $30 \times 10 =$

  c $10 \times 40 =$ **d** $0 \times 10 =$

  e $100 \times 0 =$ **f** $10 \times 10 =$

  g $10 \times 100 =$ **h** $9 \times 10 =$

6 Do these in your head. Write the answer only.

  a $10 \div 10 =$ **b** $500 \div 100 =$

  c $80 \div 10 =$ **d** $300 \div 10 =$

  e $80 \times$ $= 800$ **f** $\times 6 = 600$

  g $7000 \div 10 =$ **h** $1000 \div 1000 =$

Ma 2, Level 4   **Place value. Multiplying & dividing by 10 or 100**

Number and algebra

Test 1 Series 2   **Level Description element** Pupils use their understanding of place value to multiply and divide whole numbers by 10 or 100.

7 What is the value of the 5 in these numbers?

a 523 → 5 (   )   **b** 3751 → 5 (   )

c 615,230 → 5 (   )   **d** 5,179,320 → 5 (   )

8 Write the number which is:

a 1 more than 4000

(   )

b 10 more than 657

(   )

c 100 more than 2000

(   )

d 1000 more than 36,217

(   )

9 Write the number which is:

a 10 less than 800

(   )

b 1 less than 1000

(   )

c 100 less than 8765

(   )

d 1000 less than 2660

(   )

10

a 4000 = (   ) tens   **b** 6000 = (   ) hundreds

c 1 million = (   ) thousands   **d** 291,600 = (   ) hundreds

11 Write the answer only.

a 13 × 10 = (   )

b 72 × 100 = (   )

12 Write the answer only.

a 322 × 10 = (   )

b 441 × 100 = (   )

13 A small paint-brush costs 70p, so:

a 10 paint-brushes cost (   )

b 100 paint-brushes cost (   )

14 A box of 100 postcards costs £11, so:

a 1 postcard costs (   )

b 1000 postcards cost (   )

Name　　　　　　　　　　　　　　　　　**Date**

Mental recall of multiplication facts to 10 × 10

Level Description element In solving number problems, pupils use a range of mental and written methods of computation with the four operations, including mental recall of multiplication facts up to 10 × 10.

1 Do these in your head. Write the answers only.

$8 \times 5 =$	$6 \times 4 =$	$4 \times 5 =$
$5 \times 7 =$	$2 \times 7 =$	$4 \times 7 =$
$3 \times 2 =$	$9 \times 8 =$	$6 \times 5 =$
$3 \times 4 =$	$5 \times 3 =$	$6 \times 8 =$
$6 \times 3 =$	$7 \times 8 =$	$3 \times 9 =$
$5 \times 9 =$	$6 \times 9 =$	$8 \times 8 =$
$7 \times 6 =$	$7 \times 5 =$	$7 \times 4 =$
$8 \times 9 =$	$8 \times 3 =$	$3 \times 8 =$
$4 \times 6 =$	$4 \times 8 =$	$5 \times 6 =$
$4 \times 10 =$	$5 \times 8 =$	$5 \times 4 =$
$1 \times 8 =$	$6 \times 7 =$	$7 \times 7 =$
$7 \times 2 =$	$9 \times 9 =$	$8 \times 6 =$
$9 \times 3 =$	$9 \times 5 =$	$9 \times 4 =$
$9 \times 6 =$	$5 \times 5 =$	$4 \times 9 =$
$3 \times 3 =$	$7 \times 3 =$	$3 \times 5 =$
$3 \times 6 =$	$8 \times 7 =$	$4 \times 3 =$
$8 \times 4 =$	$3 \times 7 =$	$7 \times 9 =$
$6 \times 6 =$	$4 \times 4 =$	$9 \times 7 =$

Mathscheck	**Name**		**Date**

Ma 2, Level 4

Number and algebra

Test 3 Series 2

Adding numbers with up to three digits

Level Description element In solving number problems, pupils use a range of mental and written methods of computation with the four operations, including mental recall of multiplication facts up to 10×10.

1 a
$$\begin{array}{r} 42 \\ + \ 7 \\ \hline \end{array}$$

b
$$\begin{array}{r} 56 \\ + \ 7 \\ \hline \end{array}$$

c
$$\begin{array}{r} 28 \\ + 18 \\ \hline \end{array}$$

2 a
$$\begin{array}{r} 35 \\ + 96 \\ \hline \end{array}$$

b
$$\begin{array}{r} 263 \\ + \ 6 \\ \hline \end{array}$$

c
$$\begin{array}{r} 517 \\ + \ 8 \\ \hline \end{array}$$

3 a
$$\begin{array}{r} 261 \\ + 27 \\ \hline \end{array}$$

b
$$\begin{array}{r} 654 \\ + 36 \\ \hline \end{array}$$

c
$$\begin{array}{r} 175 \\ + 62 \\ \hline \end{array}$$

4 a
$$\begin{array}{r} 479 \\ + 65 \\ \hline \end{array}$$

b
$$\begin{array}{r} 427 \\ + 232 \\ \hline \end{array}$$

c
$$\begin{array}{r} 346 \\ + 628 \\ \hline \end{array}$$

5 a
$$\begin{array}{r} 565 \\ + 283 \\ \hline \end{array}$$

b
$$\begin{array}{r} 396 \\ + 285 \\ \hline \end{array}$$

c
$$\begin{array}{r} 588 \\ + 625 \\ \hline \end{array}$$

One sheet only

Mathscheck	**Name**	**Date**

Ma 2, Level 4

Number and algebra

Test 4 Series 2

Subtracting numbers with up to three digits

Level Description element In solving number problems, pupils use a range of mental and written methods of computation with the four operations, including mental recall of multiplication facts up to 10×10.

1 a
$$\begin{array}{r} 58 \\ -\ 26 \\ \hline \end{array}$$

b
$$\begin{array}{r} 73 \\ -\ 36 \\ \hline \end{array}$$

2 a
$$\begin{array}{r} 395 \\ -\ 72 \\ \hline \end{array}$$

b
$$\begin{array}{r} 592 \\ -\ 231 \\ \hline \end{array}$$

3 a
$$\begin{array}{r} 444 \\ -\ 7 \\ \hline \end{array}$$

b
$$\begin{array}{r} 272 \\ -\ 46 \\ \hline \end{array}$$

4 a
$$\begin{array}{r} 691 \\ -\ 479 \\ \hline \end{array}$$

b
$$\begin{array}{r} 558 \\ -\ 64 \\ \hline \end{array}$$

5 a
$$\begin{array}{r} 447 \\ -\ 262 \\ \hline \end{array}$$

b
$$\begin{array}{r} 615 \\ -\ 289 \\ \hline \end{array}$$

6 a
$$\begin{array}{r} 760 \\ -\ 378 \\ \hline \end{array}$$

b
$$\begin{array}{r} 607 \\ -\ 128 \\ \hline \end{array}$$

Name   **Date**

Multiplying numbers up to 100 by single-digit numbers

Level Description element In solving number problems, pupils use a range of mental and written methods of computation with the four operations, including mental recall of multiplication facts up to 10×10.

1 a
$$\begin{array}{r} 12 \\ \times\ \ 4 \\ \hline \end{array}$$

b
$$\begin{array}{r} 15 \\ \times\ \ 4 \\ \hline \end{array}$$

2 a
$$\begin{array}{r} 23 \\ \times\ \ 4 \\ \hline \end{array}$$

b
$$\begin{array}{r} 35 \\ \times\ \ 3 \\ \hline \end{array}$$

3 a
$$\begin{array}{r} 17 \\ \times\ \ 6 \\ \hline \end{array}$$

b
$$\begin{array}{r} 34 \\ \times\ \ 8 \\ \hline \end{array}$$

4 a
$$\begin{array}{r} 44 \\ \times\ \ 7 \\ \hline \end{array}$$

b
$$\begin{array}{r} 59 \\ \times\ \ 6 \\ \hline \end{array}$$

5 a
$$\begin{array}{r} 86 \\ \times\ \ 5 \\ \hline \end{array}$$

b
$$\begin{array}{r} 99 \\ \times\ \ 9 \\ \hline \end{array}$$

Name   *Date*

Dividing numbers up to 100 by single-digit numbers

Level Description element In solving number problems, pupils use a range of mental and written methods of computation with the four operations, including mental recall of multiplication facts up to 10×10.

Work out the answers to these 'division' calculations. Show the working.

1 $56 \div 8$

Answer ⬭

2 $49 \div 7$

Answer ⬭

3 $40 \div 2$

Answer ⬭

4 $90 \div 3$

Answer ⬭

5 $68 \div 2$

Answer ⬭

6 $63 \div 3$

Answer ⬭

7 $65 \div 5$

Answer ⬭

8 $96 \div 8$

Answer ⬭

9 $79 \div 6$

Answer ⬭

10 $83 \div 5$

Answer ⬭

Ma 2, Level 4   **Adding decimals to two places**

Number and algebra

Test 7 Series 2   **Level Description element** [Pupils] add and subtract decimals to two places.

1 a   3·6   **b**   5·8   **c**   2·6
        + 0·3   + 0·8   + 1·7
        ————   ————   ————

2 a   5·8   **b**   2·84   **c**   3·48
        + 6·5   + 0·05   + 0·06
        ————   ————   ————

3 a   3·34   **b**   7·29   **c**   2·83
        + 0·33   + 0·28   + 0·42
        ————   ————   ————

4 a   3·97   **b**   2·41   **c**   3·28
        + 0·56   + 1·26   + 6·46
        ————   ————   ————

5 a   5·73   **b**   4·85   **c**   7·77
        + 1·74   + 1·96   + 6·66
        ————   ————   ————

Name   **Date**

Subtracting decimals to two places
Level Description element [Pupils] add and subtract decimals to two places.

1 a
$$\begin{array}{r} 6\cdot7 \\ -\ 3\cdot4 \\ \hline \end{array}$$

b
$$\begin{array}{r} 8\cdot2 \\ -\ 2\cdot7 \\ \hline \end{array}$$

2 a
$$\begin{array}{r} 4\cdot59 \\ -\ 0\cdot27 \\ \hline \end{array}$$

b
$$\begin{array}{r} 6\cdot78 \\ -\ 2\cdot63 \\ \hline \end{array}$$

3 a
$$\begin{array}{r} 5\cdot55 \\ -\ 0\cdot08 \\ \hline \end{array}$$

b
$$\begin{array}{r} 3\cdot84 \\ -\ 0\cdot59 \\ \hline \end{array}$$

4 a
$$\begin{array}{r} 5\cdot73 \\ -\ 2\cdot28 \\ \hline \end{array}$$

b
$$\begin{array}{r} 4\cdot72 \\ -\ 0\cdot91 \\ \hline \end{array}$$

5 a
$$\begin{array}{r} 3\cdot68 \\ -\ 1\cdot83 \\ \hline \end{array}$$

b
$$\begin{array}{r} 5\cdot23 \\ -\ 2\cdot78 \\ \hline \end{array}$$

6 a
$$\begin{array}{r} 6\cdot20 \\ -\ 1\cdot87 \\ \hline \end{array}$$

b
$$\begin{array}{r} 7\cdot02 \\ -\ 3\cdot84 \\ \hline \end{array}$$

Rounding & approximating. Interpreting calculator displays

Level Description element In solving problems with or without a calculator, pupils check the reasonableness of their results by reference to their knowledge of the context or to the size of the numbers.

---

1 Round these numbers to the nearest 10.

  a 73

  b 395

  c 26,599

2 Round these numbers to the nearest 100.

  a 943

  b 2650

  c 37,166

---

3 Round these numbers to the nearest 1000.

  a 3678

  b 23,195

  c 621,219

4 Round these numbers to the nearest whole number.

  a 8·3

  b 77·5

  c 2391·6

---

5 Choose and ring the 'best guess' of the answer to these calculations.

a	342 + 277	590	620	650	680
b	1722 + 3665	5000	5100	5200	5400
c	743 – 376	350	370	390	400
d	3500 – 578	2600	2700	2800	2900

---

6 A pad of 100 sheets of card is 2·4 cm thick.

Use a calculator

  a   1 sheet has a thickness of [ ] mm

  b   225 sheets have a thickness of [ ] cm

---

7 Write the missing numbers in these 'chains'.

Use a calculator

  a   6   (– 2·5) = (×) = 10·5 (+ 9·9) =

  b   5·3   (+) = 7·9 (+ 0·2) = (÷ 9) =

     0·4   (÷) = 0·1 (× 10) = (+ 8·2) =

Mathscheck	**Name**		**Date**
Ma 2, Level 4	**Rounding & approximating. Interpreting calculator displays**		
Number and algebra **Test 9 Series 2**	**Level Description element** In solving problems with or without a calculator, pupils check the reasonableness of their results by reference to their knowledge of the context or to the size of the numbers.		

8 Round each of the calculator displays to the **nearest whole number.**

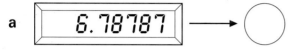

a *6.78787* ⟶ ◯   b *3.030303* ⟶ ◯

c *0.9999* ⟶ ◯   d *2.4455* ⟶ ◯

9 Use a calculator. Write the calculator answer **and** round it to the **nearest whole number.**

	calculator	to the nearest whole number
a 37·19 + 48·93		
b 81·77 − 18·88		
c 9 × 0·77		
d 92·5 ÷ 5		

10 A family gets 7 newspapers each week, each costing 37p. The bill comes every 4 weeks. What is the total bill to the **nearest** £1?

£ ☐

11 What length of wood is left if four pieces measuring 1 m 37 cm, 2 m 98 cm, 77 cm and 3 m 50 cm are cut from a plank 10 metres long? (Answer in metres.)

☐ m

12 Wire netting is sold **only** in full 1 metre lengths. How many metres must I buy to enclose this triangular rabbit run?

2 m 25 cm   2 m 25 cm

3 m 5 cm

☐ m

Ma 2, Level 4
Number and algebra
Test 10 Series 2

Fractions & percentages to describe proportions

Level Description element [Pupils] recognise approximate proportions of a whole and use simple fractions and percentages to describe these.

1 Shade $\frac{3}{8}$.

2 Shade $\frac{4}{5}$.

3
Mark and label these points on the road from X to Y.

X ——————————————— Y

L is about $\frac{2}{3}$ of the distance from X to Y.

M is about $\frac{1}{4}$ of the distance from X to Y.

N is about $\frac{3}{4}$ of the distance from X to Y.

4
Mark and label these points on the road from X to Y.

X ——————————————— Y

T is about $\frac{1}{5}$ of the distance from X to Y.

U is about $\frac{3}{10}$ of the distance from X to Y.

V is about $\frac{4}{5}$ of the distance from X to Y.

5 Shade 0·39 of this rectangle.

6 Shade 46% of this rectangle.

7 What percentage of the shape is:

a black ⬭ %

b white ⬭ %

8 In a box of 80 pencils 20 are broken.
What **percentage** are broken?

⬭ %

9 In a class of 25 children, 10 are boys.
What **percentage** are **girls?**

⬭ %

Name   **Date**

Number patterns & related terminology

Level Description element Pupils explore and describe number patterns, and relationships including multiple, factor and square.

1 In this set of numbers a line of four has been ringed.

Explain why they make a number pattern.

_____

_____

_____

_____

_____

2	3	4	5	6
12	13	14	15	16
22	23	24	25	26
32	33	34	35	36
42	43	44	45	46

2 Look carefully at this set of numbers.

Ring four numbers in a line which make a pattern.

Explain why they make a number pattern.

_____

_____

_____

_____

4	8	12	16	20
8	16	24	32	40
12	24	36	48	60
16	32	48	64	80
20	40	60	80	100

Mathscheck	Name	Date

Ma 2, Level 4
Number and algebra
Test 11 Series 2

Number patterns & related terminology
Level Description element Pupils explore and describe number patterns, and relationships including multiple, factor and square.

3 Look at these patterns of matchsticks.

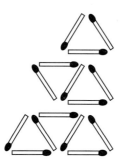

3 matchsticks

5 matchsticks

7 matchsticks

a Draw the next pattern.

b Write the next number.

c Write sentences about the patterns of shapes and numbers.

_____

_____

_____

_____

4 Complete these 'doubling and halving' patterns.

a $1 \times 48 = 2 \times$ ☐ $=$ ☐ $\times 12 = 8 \times$ ☐

b $3 \times 36 = 6 \times$ ☐ $=$ ☐ $\times 9$

5 If $14 \times 24 = 336$ which three of these number statements are true? (Tick your choices.)

a $336 \div 14 = 24$

b $14 + 24 = 336$

c $24 \times 14 = 336$

d $336 \div 24 = 14$

e $24 \div 14 = 336$

Name   **Date**

Number patterns & related terminology

Level Description element Pupils explore and describe number patterns, and relationships including multiple, factor and square.

Write the missing numbers.

6

1,   3,   5,   7,   ◯ ,   ◯

7

5,   10,   15,   ◯ ,   ◯   ,   30

8

20,   16,   12,   ◯ ,   ◯   ,   0

9

403,   402,   401,   ⬭ ,   ⬭

10

52,   49,   46,   ◯ ,   ◯

11

80,   40,   ◯ ,   10,   ◯

12

3,   6,   12,   24,   ◯ ,   ◯

13

2,   4,   7,   11,   ◯ ,   ◯

14 Look at these numbers.

18   8   30   90   40   45

Write those which are:

a multiples of 2   ◯ ◯ ◯ ◯ ◯

b multiples of 10   ◯ ◯ ◯

c multiples of 5   ◯ ◯ ◯ ◯

d multiples of 2 **and** 5   ◯ ◯ ◯

e multiples of 2 **and** 10   ◯ ◯ ◯

15 Complete this statement:

The **factors** of 36 are [   ]

Name   **Date**

Using simple formulae expressed in words

Level Description element [Pupils] have begun to use simple formulae expressed in words.

---

1 Write the missing numbers.

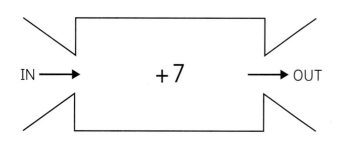

IN	OUT
5	
8	
	17
	20

---

2 Write the missing numbers.

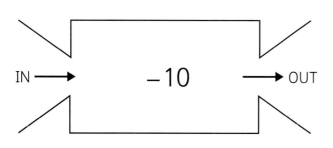

IN	OUT
21	
18	
	5
	9

---

3 Write the missing numbers.

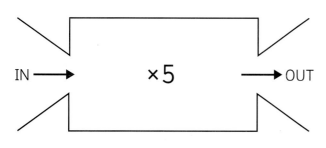

IN	OUT
4	
6	
	35
	50

---

4 Write the missing numbers.

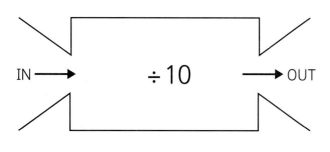

IN	OUT
60	
30	
	7
	9

Mathscheck	**Name**	**Date**
Ma 2, Level 4	**Using simple formulae expressed in words**	
Number and algebra	Level Description element [Pupils] have begun to use simple formulae expressed in words.	
Test 12 Series 2		

5 Write the missing numbers in the OUT column.

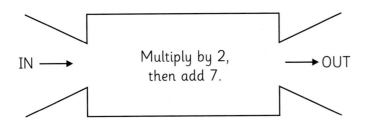

IN	OUT
2	
5	
7	

6 Write the missing numbers in the IN column.

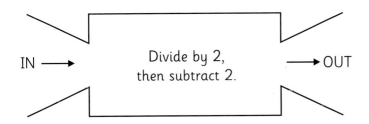

IN	OUT
	2
	5
	7

7 Write the missing numbers.

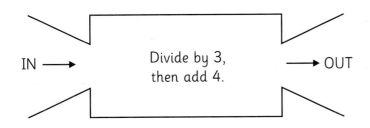

IN	OUT
9	
	8
21	

8 Look at these numbers.   Write the rule which changes the IN numbers to OUT numbers.

IN	OUT
2	10
3	12
5	16

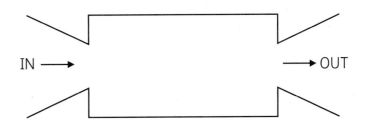

Mathscheck

Name   **Date**

Ma 2, Level 4
Number and algebra
Test 12 Series 2

Using simple formulae expressed in words
Level Description element [Pupils] have begun to use simple formulae expressed in words.

9 I add 2 to a number, then multiply the result by 5. The answer is 30.
What number did I start with?

I started with ⬭

10 I halve a number, then add 2 and the result is 16.
What is the number I started with?

I started with ⬭

11 Write the missing number.

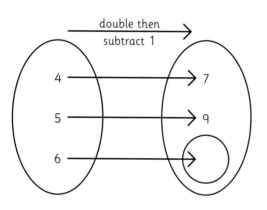

12 Write the missing number.

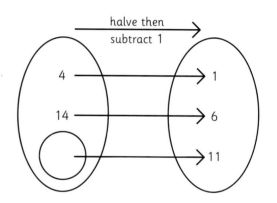

13 Complete the rule.

Week	1	2	3	4	5	6				
Total amount saved	20 p	40 p	60 p	80 p	£1	£1·20				

Rule:

Total amount saved = number of ⬭ × ⬭ p

14 Complete the rule.

Jen's age	4	5	6	7	8	9				
Ali's age	7	8	9	10	11	12				

Rule:

Jen's age = ☐ 's age − ⬭

Ma 2, Level 4

Number and algebra

Test 13 Series 2

Using & interpreting co-ordinates in the first quadrant

Level Description element Pupils use and interpret co-ordinates in the first quadrant.

1 Plot these co-ordinates, then join them in the same order to draw a shape.

a
(3,6)
(6,6)
(4,1)
(1,1)
(3,6)

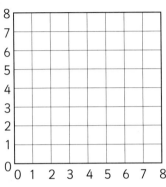

b
(2,1)
(5,1)
(7,4)
(5,7)
(2,7)
(0,4)
(2,1)

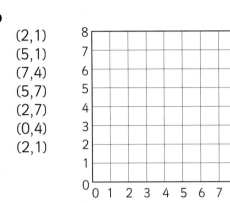

c
(7,2)
(3,2)
(3,6)
(7,6)
(7,2)

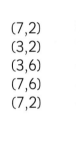

d
(7,3)
(7,5)
(5,7)
(3,7)
(1,5)
(1,3)
(3,1)
(5,1)
(7,3)

e
(0,2)
(3,4)
(6,2)
(3,7)
(0,2)

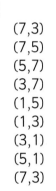

f
(0,0)
(5,2)
(5,5)
(2,5)
(0,0)

g
(6,5)
(1,7)
(1,1)
(6,3)
(6,5)

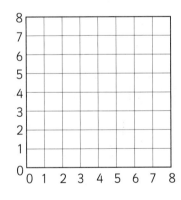

h
(2,4)
(4,6)
(6,4)
(4,2)
(2,4)

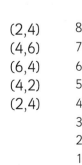

Name   **Date**

Constructing simple 3-D models from nets

Level Description element Pupils make 3-D mathematical models by linking given faces or edges, draw common 2-D shapes in different orientations on grids, and identify congruent shapes and orders of rotational symmetry.

1 Use centimetre squared paper, scissors, ruler, pencil and glue.
  a On the squared paper, draw the **nets** to make each shape.
  b Construct the 3-D shape from the net, full size.

  Look carefully at the measurements!

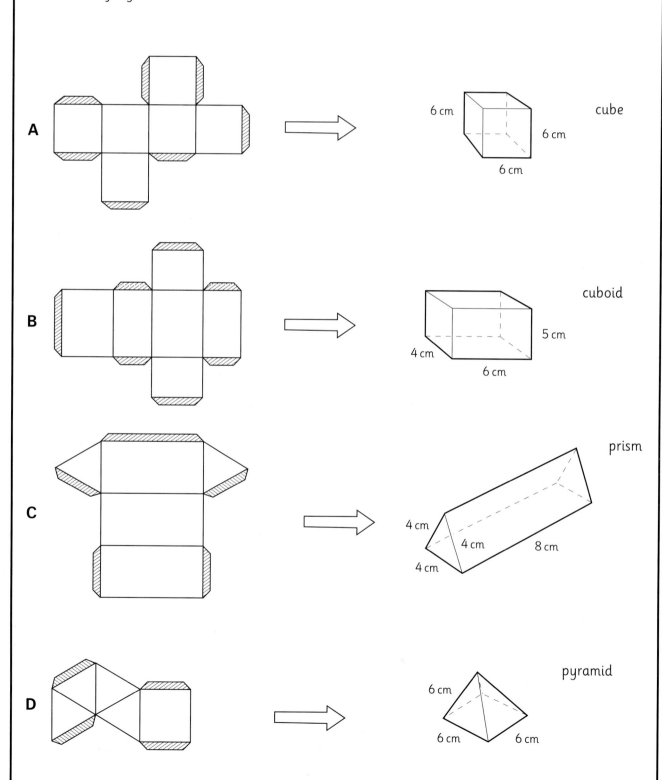

A   6 cm   6 cm   6 cm   cube

B   5 cm   4 cm   6 cm   cuboid

C   4 cm   4 cm   8 cm   4 cm   prism

D   6 cm   6 cm   6 cm   pyramid

Ma 3, Level 4

Shape, space and measures

Test 15 Series 2

Constructing 2-D shapes & identifying congruence

Level Description element Pupils make 3-D mathematical models by linking given faces or edges, draw common 2-D shapes in different orientations on grids, and identify congruent shapes and orders of rotational symmetry.

You need: compasses, ruler, sharp pencil, set square.

1 Join the angle to the correct name.

(right angle)   (reflex angle)   (acute angle)   (obtuse angle)

2 Draw a line which is **parallel** to the line PQ.

3 Draw a **diagonal** on this shape.

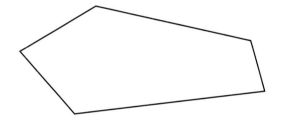

4 Draw a line from X, which is **perpendicular** to the line AB.

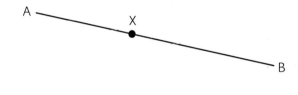

5 a Draw a **square** of side 3·5 cm.

  b Mark its **centre** with a cross and label it M.

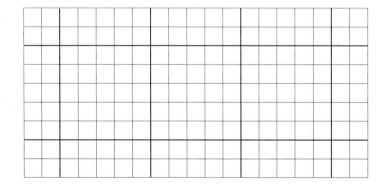

6 a Draw a **rectangle** measuring 7·5 cm by 4·5 cm.

  b Mark its **centre** with a cross and label it M.

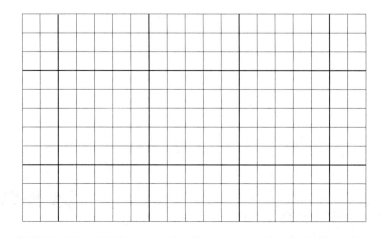

Name   **Date**

Constructing 2-D shapes & identifying congruence

Level Description element Pupils make 3-D mathematical models by linking given faces or edges, draw common 2-D shapes in different orientations on grids, and identify congruent shapes and orders of rotational symmetry.

7 a Draw a circle of radius 2 cm.
   b Draw a diameter on it.

8 Use a pair of compasses, a ruler and a pencil.
Bisect this angle.

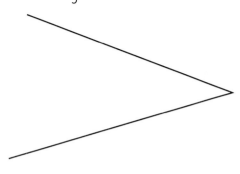

9 Use a pair of compasses, a ruler and a pencil.
Draw this triangle full size.

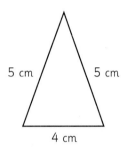

5 cm   5 cm

4 cm

10 Use a pair of compasses, a ruler and a pencil.
Draw this triangle full size.

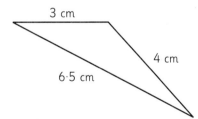

3 cm

4 cm

6·5 cm

11 Join pairs of **congruent** shapes.

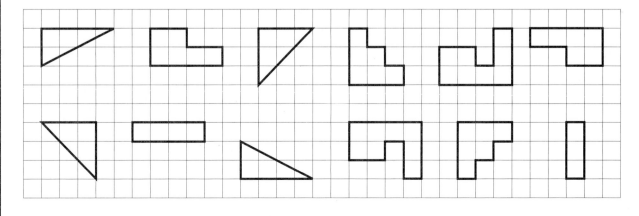

Mathscheck

Ma 3, Level 4

Shape, space
and measures

Test 16 Series 2

Name   **Date**

Identifying orders of rotational symmetry

Level Description element Pupils make 3-D mathematical models by linking given faces or edges, draw common 2-D shapes in different orientations on grids, and identify congruent shapes and orders of rotational symmetry.

1 Write on each shape its order of rotational symmetry.

Use tracing paper to help you to decide.

a

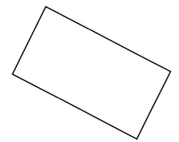

b

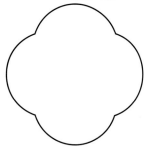

c

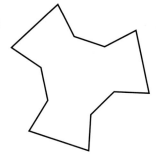

d

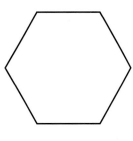

e

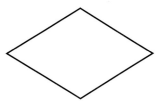

f

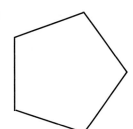

g

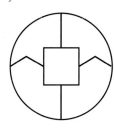

2 This is $\frac{1}{4}$ of a shape. Use tracing paper to help you finish it to make a shape with rotational symmetry of order 4.

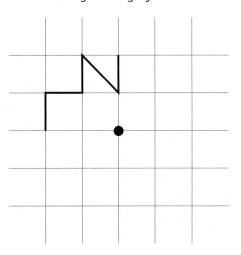

3 Ring the letters which have rotational symmetry of order two or more.

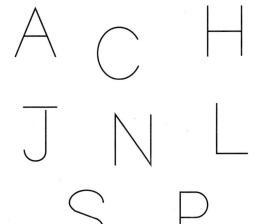

Name   **Date**

Reflecting simple shapes in a mirror line

Level Description element [Pupils] reflect simple shapes in a mirror line.

1 Reflect the designs in the mirror lines to show 2-D symmetrical shapes.

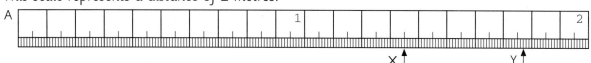

Ma 3, Level 4

Shape, space
and measures

Test 18 Series 2

Interpreting numbers on measuring instruments

Level Description element [Pupils] choose and use appropriate units and instruments, interpreting, with appropriate accuracy, numbers on a range of measuring instruments.

1 This scale represents a distance of 2 metres.

A

X ↑   Y ↑

Write in **decimal form** the measurement from A shown by the arrows.

X is (⬭) metres from A.   Y is (⬭) metres from A.

2 Write the times shown in digital form.

a    (⬭)

b 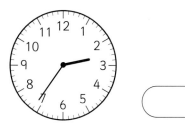   (⬭)

3 Write the weights shown on the scales.

a 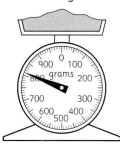   (⬭)

b 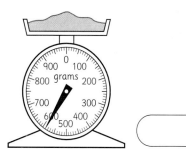   (⬭)

4 Write the the amount of liquid in each container.

a 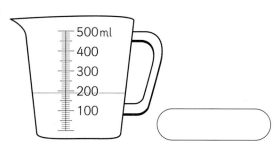   (⬭)

b 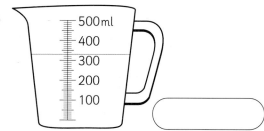   (⬭)

5 Write the size of these angles.

a 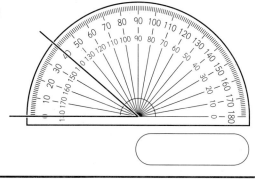   (⬭)

b 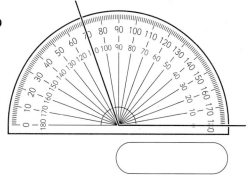   (⬭)

Finding perimeters, areas & volumes by counting

Level Description element [Pupils] find perimeters of simple shapes, find areas by counting squares, and find volumes by counting cubes.

1 What is the **perimeter** of each shape?

Hint: they are drawn on 1 cm grids.

a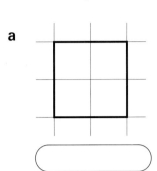

b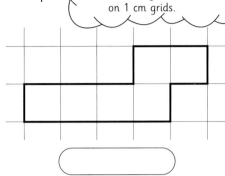

c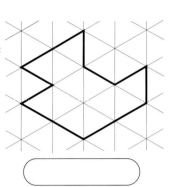

2 Calculate the **perimeter** of each shape.   (Not drawn to scale.)

a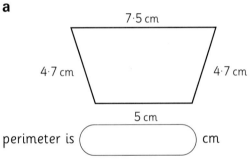

7·5 cm

4·7 cm   4·7 cm

5 cm

perimeter is (   ) cm

b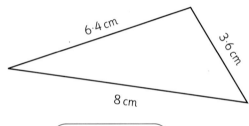

6·4 cm

3·6 cm

8 cm

perimeter is (   ) cm

3 Draw a shape with a **perimeter** of 16 cm.

4 Write the **area** of each shape (in cm²).

a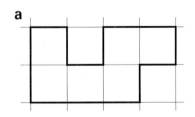

Area is cm²

b

Area is [   ] cm²

5 Write the **area** of each shape (in cm²).

a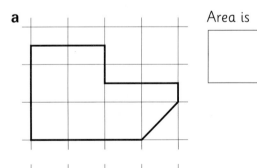

Area is [   ] cm²

b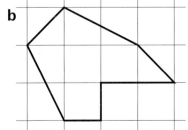

Area is [   ] cm²

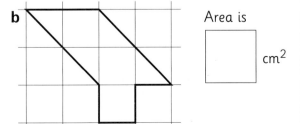

Mathscheck

Ma 3, Level 4

Shape, space and measures

Test 19 Series 2

Finding perimeters, areas & volumes by counting

Level Description element [Pupils] find perimeters of simple shapes, find areas by counting squares, and find volumes by counting cubes.

Name   Date

6 Find the approximate **area** of this shape (in cm²).

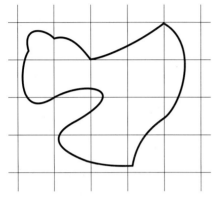

Approximate area is

cm²

7 Draw a shape with an **area** of $9\frac{1}{2}$ cm².

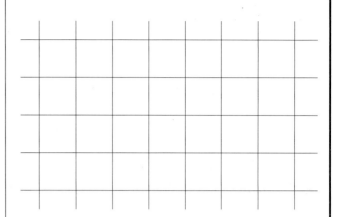

8 These shapes are made using centimetre cubes. Count the cubes to find the **volume** of each shape:

Note that some cubes are hidden behind others.

a

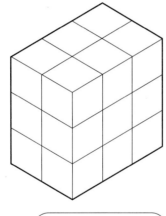

Volume is (   ) cm³

b

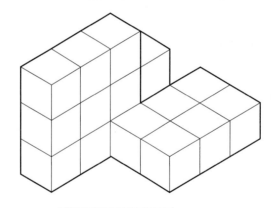

Volume is (   ) cm³

9 These shapes use centimetre cubes, and some have been cut in half. Find the **volume** of each shape:

a

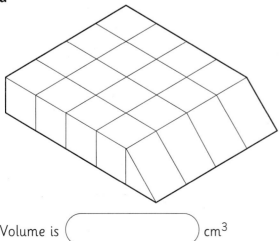

Volume is (   ) cm³

b

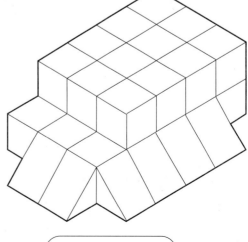

Volume is (   ) cm³

Name   **Date**

Collecting & recording data

Level Description element Pupils collect discrete data and record them using a frequency table.

1 Choose a topic for which data would have to be collected. Write its title here.

2 Use this grid to help you draw a tally chart or frequency table. Use your chart or table to record your data.

3 Draw a chart or graph of your data on this grid.

Name   **Date**

Recognising & using the mode & median
Level Description element [Pupils] understand and use the mode and median.

---

1 Write the **mode** of each set of numbers.

a 5 4 5 6 5 5 6   Mode is ( )

b 9 5 9 7 9 6 5 9 9 5   Mode is ( )

c 7·5 8·2 8·1 7·5 8·2 7·5   Mode is ( )
     7·5 8·2 7·5

---

2 Write the **median** of each set of numbers.

a 7 6 7 6 8   Median is ( )

b 6 6 7 7 7 7 8   Median is ( )

c 2·31 2·40 2·25 2·34   Median is ( )
     2·51 2·29 2·36

---

3 This table shows the shoe sizes of 30 children in a class.

Leroy	5	Helen	$3\frac{1}{2}$	Moshe	$4\frac{1}{2}$
Mary	$5\frac{1}{2}$	Tom	$4\frac{1}{2}$	Miriam	5
Marlene	7	Sarah	$6\frac{1}{2}$	Norma	$4\frac{1}{2}$
Alan	5	Indira	1	Cyril	$4\frac{1}{2}$
Ali	$4\frac{1}{2}$	Jean	$3\frac{1}{2}$	Azil	$5\frac{1}{2}$
Diane	$2\frac{1}{2}$	Lucy	2	Jafar	$3\frac{1}{2}$
Ewen	6	Justin	4	Lisa	$6\frac{1}{2}$
Colin	$4\frac{1}{2}$	Danielle	$4\frac{1}{2}$	Katy	$4\frac{1}{2}$
Penny	4	Peter	3	Tarun	4
Pablo	3	Fatima	$1\frac{1}{2}$	Rajindar	2

a Complete this table of the shoe sizes.

Shoe size	1	$1\frac{1}{2}$	2	$2\frac{1}{2}$	3	$3\frac{1}{2}$	4	$4\frac{1}{2}$	5	$5\frac{1}{2}$	6	$6\frac{1}{2}$	7
Number of children													

b The median shoe size is ( )

c The modal shoe size is ( )

Representing & interpreting data in equal class intervals

Level Description element [Pupils] group data, where appropriate, in equal class intervals, represent collected data in frequency diagrams and interpret such diagrams.

1 In a competition to see how many items you could fit into a matchbox, these were the results:

7	11	12	15	18	19	15	14	10	6	14	15	20
10	8	11	14	17	18	19	16	14	10	9	17	20
13	20	19	16	9	16	17						

a Complete this tally chart of the data.

Number of items	Tally	Frequency
6 – 8		
9 – 11		
12 – 14		
15 – 17		
18 – 20		

b Draw a frequency diagram of the results on this grid.

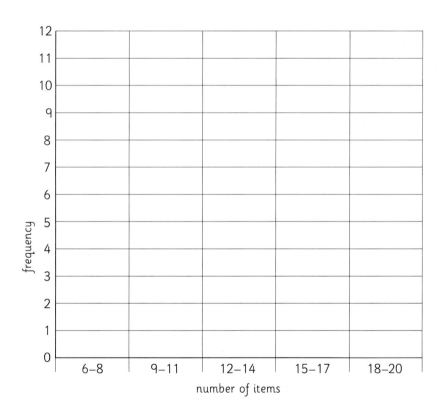

c Complete these statements about the data.

The median is ⟨　　　　⟩   The mode is ⟨　　　　⟩

Ma 4, Level 4

Handling data

Test 23 Series 2

Constructing & interpreting simple line graphs

Level Description element [Pupils] construct and interpret simple line graphs.

1 Draw a bar-line graph of this data.

Ice cream sold in the week	
Day	Frequency (Numbers sold)
Sunday	10
Monday	22
Tuesday	15
Wednesday	24
Thursday	6
Friday	18
Saturday	20

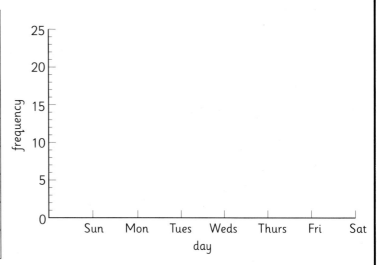

2 Answer the questions about this line graph of temperatures.

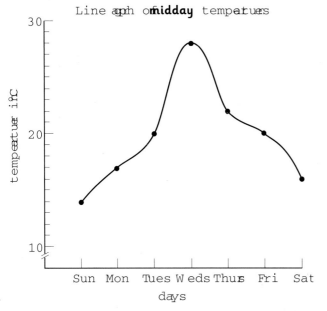

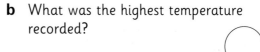

a What was the lowest temperature recorded? ◯ °C

b What was the highest temperature recorded? ◯ °C

c What was the range of temperatures recorded? ◯ °C

d What does the graph show as the approximate temperature at **midnight** between Sunday and Monday? ◯ °C

e Write why this is only a guess at the temperature at midnight.

Mathscheck | **Name** | **Date**

Ma 4, Level 4 | **Probability: certainty & uncertainty, likelihood & fairness**

Handling data

Test 24 Series 2 | **Level Description element** [Pupils] understand and use simple vocabulary associated with probability, including 'fair', 'certain' and 'likely'.

Tick the correct word.

1 You will be 100 years old tomorrow:

certain
uncertain
impossible

2 £1 is more than 1p:

certain
uncertain
impossible

3 It will be salad for tea today:

certain
uncertain
impossible

4 The first cube you take from the box will be blue:

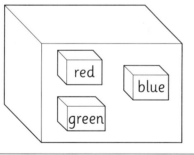

certain
uncertain
impossible

5 Today you will meet a dog as tall as your house:

certain
uncertain
impossible

6 You will watch a film about tigers today:

certain
uncertain
impossible

Name

Date

Probability: certainty & uncertainty, likelihood & fairness

Level Description element [Pupils] understand and use simple vocabulary associated with probability, including 'fair', 'certain' and 'likely'.

7 Are these events **more likely** or **less likely** to happen?
Write 'more' or 'less' in the correct spaces.

( ) likely   ( ) likely

( ) likely   ( ) likely

8 A box of mixed crayons has these numbers of different colours.

Colour	Number
black	25
green	7
orange	12
blue	19

I close my eyes and pick out one crayon.
a Which colour am I **least likely** to pick out? ( )
b Write why you chose that colour.

c Which colour am I **most likely** to pick out? ( )

9 Are these events | **very likely** | , | **likely** | , | **unlikely** | or | **very unlikely** | to happen?

a You will get £100 pocket money next week. ( )

b A new girl will join your class next year. ( )

c You will find 10 p outside school today. ( )

d There will be a cloud in the sky on Monday. ( )

Probability: certainty & uncertainty, likelihood & fairness

Level Description element [Pupils] understand and use simple vocabulary associated with probability, including 'fair', 'certain' and 'likely'.

10 Look at this spinner.

After spinning the pointer:

a the **least likely** result is

b the **most likely** result is

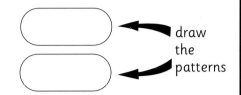

draw the patterns

11 Colour these spinners so that the result of a spin:

a is **unlikely** to point to green

b is **certain** to point to blue

c has an **even chance** of pointing to red or yellow

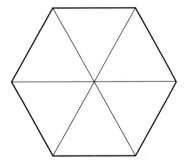

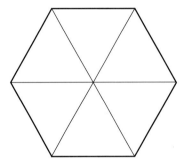

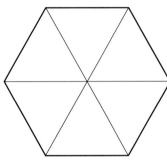

d is **likely** to point to red

e has **no chance** of pointing to red

f is **equally likely** to point to brown, red and blue

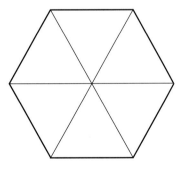

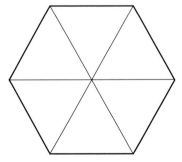

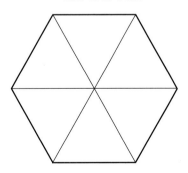

12 Are these dice games **fair** or **unfair**?

a Tariq has to roll a 6 to win.
Sonia has to roll a 1 to win.

b Eric has to roll an even number to win.
Lucy has to roll an odd number to win.

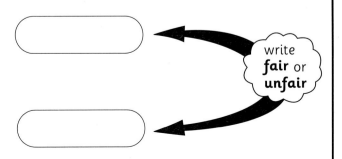

write **fair** or **unfair**

Answers for Level 4

Mathscheck — Name / Date

Ma 2, Level 4 — Number and algebra — Test 1 Series 2

Place value. Multiplying & dividing by 10 or 100

Level Description element Pupils use their understanding of place value to multiply and divide whole numbers by 10 or 100.

1 Write in numerals:

a six hundred and eight — 608

b sixteen thousand and four — 16,004

c three million — 3,000,000

d two hundred and four thousand and five — 204,005

2 Write in words:

a 409 — four hundred and nine

b 2929 — two thousand nine hundred and twenty-nine

c 61,030 — sixty one thousand and thirty

3 Write these numbers in ascending order: 3412 40,123 12,340 1430 23,140

1430   3412   12,340   23,140   40,123

4 Use only these digits 5 7 1 1 3. Change the order to make:

a the smallest number — 11,357

b the largest number — 75,311

5 Do these in your head. Write the answer only.

a $10 \times 1 = 10$

b $30 \times 10 = 300$

c $10 \times 40 = 400$

d $0 \times 10 = 0$

e $100 \times 0 = 0$

f $10 \times 10 = 100$

g $10 \times 100 = 1000$

h $9 \times 10 = 90$

6 Do these in your head. Write the answer only.

a $10 \div 10 = 1$

b $500 \div 100 = 5$

c $80 \div 10 = 8$

d $300 \div 10 = 30$

e $80 \times 10 = 800$

f $100 \times 6 = 600$

g $7000 \div 10 = 700$

h $1000 \div 1000 = 1$

Mathscheck — Name / Date

Ma 2, Level 4 — Number and algebra — Test 1 Series 1

Place value. Multiplying & dividing by 10 or 100

Level Description element Pupils use their understanding of place value to multiply and divide whole numbers by 10 or 100.

1 Write in numerals:

a seven hundred and five — 705

b seventeen thousand and seventeen — 17,017

c one million — 1,000,000

d one hundred and six thousand and twenty-one — 106,021

2 Write in words:

a 222 — two hundred and twenty-two

b 4685 — four thousand six hundred and eighty-five

c 30,035 — thirty thousand and thirty-five

3 Write these numbers in descending order: 12,603 2613 16,302 632 12,360

16,302   12,603   12,360   2613   632

4 Use only these digits 3 4 7 1 2. Change the order to make:

a the largest number — 74,321

b the smallest number — 12,347

5 Do these in your head. Write the answer only.

a $5 \times 10 = 50$

b $1 \times 10 = 10$

c $10 \times 0 = 0$

d $20 \times 10 = 200$

e $50 \times 10 = 500$

f $100 \times 10 = 1000$

g $10 \times 10 = 100$

h $0 \times 100 = 0$

6 Do these in your head. Write the answer only.

a $90 \div 10 = 9$

b $10 \div 10 = 1$

c $600 \div 10 = 60$

d $700 \div 100 = 7$

e $40 \times 10 = 400$

f $100 \times 7 = 700$

g $1000 \div 10 = 100$

h $5000 \div 100 = 50$

Ma 2, Level 4
Number and algebra
Test 1 Series 2

Place value. Multiplying & dividing by 10 or 100
Level Description element Pupils use their understanding of place value to multiply and divide whole numbers by 10 or 100.

7 What is the value of the 5 in these numbers?

a $523 \rightarrow 5$ (hundreds)   b $3751 \rightarrow 5$ (tens)

c $615,230 \rightarrow 5$ (thousands)   d $5,179,320 \rightarrow 5$ (millions)

8 Write the number which is:

a 1 more than 4000 (4001)   b 10 more than 657 (667)

c 100 more than 2000 (2100)   d 1000 more than 36,217 (37,217)

9 Write the number which is:

a 10 less than 800 (790)   b 1 less than 1000 (999)

c 100 less than 8765 (8665)   d 1000 less than 2660 (1660)

10

a $4000 =$ (400) tens   b $6000 =$ (60) hundreds

c 1 million $=$ (1000) thousands   d $291,600 =$ (2916) hundreds

11 Write the answer only.

a $13 \times 10 =$ (130)   b $72 \times 100 =$ (7200)

12 Write the answer only.

a $322 \times 10 =$ (3220)   b $441 \times 100 =$ (44,100)

13 A small paint-brush costs 70p, so:

a 10 paint-brushes cost (£7)   b 100 paint-brushes cost (£70)

14 A box of 100 postcards costs £11, so:

a 1 postcard costs (£0·11 or 11p)   b 1000 postcards cost (£110)

Ma 2, Level 4
Number and algebra
Test 1 Series 1

Place value. Multiplying & dividing by 10 or 100
Level Description element Pupils use their understanding of place value to multiply and divide whole numbers by 10 or 100.

7 What is the value of the 4 in these numbers?

a $243 \rightarrow 4$ (tens)   b $4567 \rightarrow 4$ (thousands)

c $4,111,222 \rightarrow 4$ (millions)   d $234,211 \rightarrow 4$ (thousands)

8 Write the number which is:

a 10 more than 595 (605)   b 100 more than 757 (857)

c 1 more than 2000 (2001)   d 1000 more than 24,132 (25,132)

9 Write the number which is:

a 1 less than 700 (699)   b 10 less than 2000 (1990)

c 100 less than 1562 (1462)   d 1000 less than 1624 (624)

10

a $3000 =$ (30) hundreds   b $2500 =$ (250) tens

c $132,400 =$ (1324) hundreds   d 2 million $=$ (2000) thousands

11 Write the answer only.

a $10 \times 18 =$ (180)   b $100 \times 36 =$ (3600)

12 Write the answer only.

a $10 \times 254 =$ (2540)   b $100 \times 555 =$ (55,500)

13 A computer disk costs 90p, so:

a 10 disks cost (£9)   b 100 disks cost (£90)

14 A box of 100 postcards costs £12, so:

a 1 postcard costs (£0·12 or 12p)   b 1000 postcards cost (£120)

Ma 2, Level 4
Number and algebra
Test 2 Series 2

Mental recall of multiplication facts to 10 × 10

Level Description element In solving number problems, pupils use a range of mental and written methods of computation with the four operations, including mental recall of multiplication facts up to 10 × 10.

1 Do these in your head. Write the answers only.

8 × 5 = 40	6 × 4 = 24	4 × 5 = 20
5 × 7 = 35	2 × 7 = 14	4 × 7 = 28
3 × 2 = 6	9 × 8 = 72	6 × 5 = 30
3 × 4 = 12	5 × 3 = 15	6 × 8 = 48
6 × 3 = 18	7 × 8 = 56	3 × 9 = 27
5 × 9 = 45	6 × 9 = 54	8 × 8 = 64
7 × 6 = 42	7 × 5 = 35	7 × 4 = 28
8 × 9 = 72	8 × 3 = 24	3 × 8 = 24
4 × 6 = 24	4 × 8 = 32	5 × 6 = 30
4 × 10 = 40	5 × 8 = 40	5 × 4 = 20
1 × 8 = 8	6 × 7 = 42	7 × 7 = 49
7 × 2 = 14	9 × 9 = 81	8 × 6 = 48
9 × 3 = 27	9 × 5 = 45	9 × 4 = 36
9 × 6 = 54	5 × 5 = 25	4 × 9 = 36
3 × 3 = 9	7 × 3 = 21	3 × 5 = 15
3 × 6 = 18	8 × 7 = 56	4 × 3 = 12
8 × 4 = 32	3 × 7 = 21	7 × 9 = 63
6 × 6 = 36	4 × 4 = 16	9 × 7 = 63

Ma 2, Level 4
Number and algebra
Test 2 Series 1

Mental recall of multiplication facts to 10 × 10

Level Description element In solving number problems, pupils use a range of mental and written methods of computation with the four operations, including mental recall of multiplication facts up to 10 × 10.

1 Do these in your head. Write the answers only.

4 × 4 = 16	6 × 6 = 36	9 × 7 = 63
3 × 7 = 21	8 × 4 = 32	7 × 9 = 63
8 × 7 = 56	3 × 6 = 18	4 × 3 = 12
7 × 3 = 21	3 × 3 = 9	3 × 5 = 15
5 × 5 = 25	9 × 6 = 54	4 × 9 = 36
9 × 5 = 45	9 × 3 = 27	9 × 4 = 36
9 × 9 = 81	7 × 2 = 14	8 × 6 = 48
6 × 7 = 42	1 × 8 = 8	7 × 7 = 49
5 × 8 = 40	4 × 10 = 40	5 × 4 = 20
4 × 8 = 32	4 × 6 = 24	5 × 6 = 30
8 × 3 = 24	8 × 9 = 72	3 × 8 = 24
7 × 5 = 35	7 × 6 = 42	7 × 4 = 28
6 × 9 = 54	5 × 9 = 45	8 × 8 = 64
7 × 8 = 56	6 × 3 = 18	3 × 9 = 27
5 × 3 = 15	3 × 4 = 12	6 × 8 = 48
9 × 8 = 72	3 × 2 = 6	6 × 5 = 30
2 × 7 = 14	5 × 7 = 35	4 × 7 = 28
6 × 4 = 24	8 × 5 = 40	4 × 5 = 20

Mathscheck — Name / Date

Adding numbers with up to three digits

Level Description element In solving number problems, pupils use a range of mental and written methods of computation with the four operations, including mental recall of multiplication facts up to 10×10.

1
a
$$\begin{array}{r} 36 \\ +\ 3 \\ \hline 39 \end{array}$$
b
$$\begin{array}{r} 58 \\ +\ 8 \\ \hline 66 \end{array}$$
c
$$\begin{array}{r} 26 \\ +\ 17 \\ \hline 43 \end{array}$$

2
a
$$\begin{array}{r} 58 \\ +\ 65 \\ \hline 123 \end{array}$$
b
$$\begin{array}{r} 284 \\ +\ 5 \\ \hline 289 \end{array}$$
c
$$\begin{array}{r} 348 \\ +\ 6 \\ \hline 354 \end{array}$$

3
a
$$\begin{array}{r} 324 \\ +\ 33 \\ \hline 357 \end{array}$$
b
$$\begin{array}{r} 729 \\ +\ 28 \\ \hline 757 \end{array}$$
c
$$\begin{array}{r} 283 \\ +\ 42 \\ \hline 325 \end{array}$$

4
a
$$\begin{array}{r} 397 \\ +\ 56 \\ \hline 453 \end{array}$$
b
$$\begin{array}{r} 241 \\ +\ 126 \\ \hline 367 \end{array}$$
c
$$\begin{array}{r} 328 \\ +\ 646 \\ \hline 974 \end{array}$$

5
a
$$\begin{array}{r} 573 \\ +\ 174 \\ \hline 747 \end{array}$$
b
$$\begin{array}{r} 485 \\ +\ 196 \\ \hline 681 \end{array}$$
c
$$\begin{array}{r} 777 \\ +\ 666 \\ \hline 1443 \end{array}$$

Mathscheck — Name / Date

Adding numbers with up to three digits

Level Description element In solving number problems, pupils use a range of mental and written methods of computation with the four operations, including mental recall of multiplication facts up to 10×10.

1
a
$$\begin{array}{r} 42 \\ +\ 7 \\ \hline 49 \end{array}$$
b
$$\begin{array}{r} 56 \\ +\ 7 \\ \hline 63 \end{array}$$
c
$$\begin{array}{r} 28 \\ +\ 18 \\ \hline 46 \end{array}$$

2
a
$$\begin{array}{r} 35 \\ +\ 96 \\ \hline 131 \end{array}$$
b
$$\begin{array}{r} 263 \\ +\ 6 \\ \hline 269 \end{array}$$
c
$$\begin{array}{r} 517 \\ +\ 8 \\ \hline 525 \end{array}$$

3
a
$$\begin{array}{r} 261 \\ +\ 27 \\ \hline 288 \end{array}$$
b
$$\begin{array}{r} 654 \\ +\ 36 \\ \hline 690 \end{array}$$
c
$$\begin{array}{r} 175 \\ +\ 62 \\ \hline 237 \end{array}$$

4
a
$$\begin{array}{r} 479 \\ +\ 65 \\ \hline 544 \end{array}$$
b
$$\begin{array}{r} 427 \\ +\ 232 \\ \hline 659 \end{array}$$
c
$$\begin{array}{r} 346 \\ +\ 628 \\ \hline 974 \end{array}$$

5
a
$$\begin{array}{r} 565 \\ +\ 283 \\ \hline 848 \end{array}$$
b
$$\begin{array}{r} 396 \\ +\ 285 \\ \hline 681 \end{array}$$
c
$$\begin{array}{r} 588 \\ +\ 625 \\ \hline 1213 \end{array}$$

Mathscheck

Ma 2, Level 4
Number and algebra
Test 4 Series 1

Name   **Date**

Subtracting numbers with up to three digits

Level Description element In solving number problems, pupils use a range of mental and written methods of computation with the four operations, including mental recall of multiplication facts up to 10 × 10.

	a	b
1	$\begin{array}{r} 67 \\ -\ 34 \\ \hline 33 \end{array}$	$\begin{array}{r} 82 \\ -\ 27 \\ \hline 55 \end{array}$
2	$\begin{array}{r} 459 \\ -\ 27 \\ \hline 432 \end{array}$	$\begin{array}{r} 678 \\ -\ 263 \\ \hline 415 \end{array}$
3	$\begin{array}{r} 555 \\ -\ 8 \\ \hline 547 \end{array}$	$\begin{array}{r} 384 \\ -\ 59 \\ \hline 325 \end{array}$
4	$\begin{array}{r} 573 \\ -\ 228 \\ \hline 345 \end{array}$	$\begin{array}{r} 472 \\ -\ 91 \\ \hline 381 \end{array}$
5	$\begin{array}{r} 368 \\ -\ 183 \\ \hline 185 \end{array}$	$\begin{array}{r} 523 \\ -\ 278 \\ \hline 245 \end{array}$
6	$\begin{array}{r} 620 \\ -\ 187 \\ \hline 433 \end{array}$	$\begin{array}{r} 702 \\ -\ 384 \\ \hline 318 \end{array}$

   One sheet only   27

Mathscheck

Ma 2, Level 4
Number and algebra
Test 4 Series 2

Name   **Date**

Subtracting numbers with up to three digits

Level Description element In solving number problems, pupils use a range of mental and written methods of computation with the four operations, including mental recall of multiplication facts up to 10 × 10.

	a	b
1	$\begin{array}{r} 58 \\ -\ 26 \\ \hline 32 \end{array}$	$\begin{array}{r} 73 \\ -\ 36 \\ \hline 37 \end{array}$
2	$\begin{array}{r} 395 \\ -\ 72 \\ \hline 323 \end{array}$	$\begin{array}{r} 592 \\ -\ 231 \\ \hline 361 \end{array}$
3	$\begin{array}{r} 444 \\ -\ 7 \\ \hline 437 \end{array}$	$\begin{array}{r} 272 \\ -\ 46 \\ \hline 226 \end{array}$
4	$\begin{array}{r} 691 \\ -\ 479 \\ \hline 212 \end{array}$	$\begin{array}{r} 558 \\ -\ 64 \\ \hline 494 \end{array}$
5	$\begin{array}{r} 447 \\ -\ 262 \\ \hline 185 \end{array}$	$\begin{array}{r} 615 \\ -\ 289 \\ \hline 326 \end{array}$
6	$\begin{array}{r} 760 \\ -\ 378 \\ \hline 382 \end{array}$	$\begin{array}{r} 607 \\ -\ 128 \\ \hline 479 \end{array}$

   One sheet only   61

Mathscheck

Ma 2, Level 4
Number and algebra
Test 5 Series 1

Multiplying numbers up to 100 by single-digit numbers
Level Description element In solving number problems, pupils use a range of mental and
written methods of computation with the four operations, including mental recall of
multiplication facts up to 10 × 10.

1 a
$$\begin{array}{r} 13 \\ \times\ 3 \\ \hline 39 \end{array}$$

b
$$\begin{array}{r} 14 \\ \times\ 5 \\ \hline 70 \end{array}$$

2 a
$$\begin{array}{r} 27 \\ \times\ 3 \\ \hline 81 \end{array}$$

b
$$\begin{array}{r} 34 \\ \times\ 3 \\ \hline 102 \end{array}$$

3 a
$$\begin{array}{r} 15 \\ \times\ 7 \\ \hline 105 \end{array}$$

b
$$\begin{array}{r} 46 \\ \times\ 7 \\ \hline 322 \end{array}$$

4 a
$$\begin{array}{r} 55 \\ \times\ 6 \\ \hline 330 \end{array}$$

b
$$\begin{array}{r} 68 \\ \times\ 7 \\ \hline 476 \end{array}$$

5 a
$$\begin{array}{r} 74 \\ \times\ 5 \\ \hline 370 \end{array}$$

b
$$\begin{array}{r} 88 \\ \times\ 8 \\ \hline 704 \end{array}$$

Mathscheck

Ma 2, Level 4
Number and algebra
Test 5 Series 2

Multiplying numbers up to 100 by single-digit numbers
Level Description element In solving number problems, pupils use a range of mental and
written methods of computation with the four operations, including mental recall of
multiplication facts up to 10 × 10.

1 a
$$\begin{array}{r} 12 \\ \times\ 4 \\ \hline 48 \end{array}$$

b
$$\begin{array}{r} 15 \\ \times\ 4 \\ \hline 60 \end{array}$$

2 a
$$\begin{array}{r} 23 \\ \times\ 4 \\ \hline 92 \end{array}$$

b
$$\begin{array}{r} 35 \\ \times\ 3 \\ \hline 105 \end{array}$$

3 a
$$\begin{array}{r} 17 \\ \times\ 6 \\ \hline 102 \end{array}$$

b
$$\begin{array}{r} 34 \\ \times\ 8 \\ \hline 272 \end{array}$$

4 a
$$\begin{array}{r} 44 \\ \times\ 7 \\ \hline 308 \end{array}$$

b
$$\begin{array}{r} 59 \\ \times\ 6 \\ \hline 354 \end{array}$$

5 a
$$\begin{array}{r} 86 \\ \times\ 5 \\ \hline 430 \end{array}$$

b
$$\begin{array}{r} 99 \\ \times\ 9 \\ \hline 891 \end{array}$$

Worksheet 1

Ma 2, Level 4
Number and algebra
Test 6 Series 2

Dividing numbers up to 100 by single-digit numbers

Level Description element In solving number problems, pupils use a range of mental and written methods of computation with the four operations, including mental recall of multiplication facts up to 10×10.

Work out the answers to these 'division' calculations. Show the working.

1 $56 \div 8$ Answer (7)

2 $49 \div 7$ Answer (7)

3 $40 \div 2$ Answer (20)

4 $90 \div 3$ Answer (30)

5 $68 \div 2$ Answer (34)

6 $63 \div 3$ Answer (21)

7 $65 \div 5$ Answer (13)

8 $96 \div 8$ Answer (12)

9 $79 \div 6$ 13·16   Answer (or 13 r1 / or $13\frac{1}{6}$)

10 $83 \div 5$ 16·6   Answer (or 16 r6 / or $16\frac{3}{5}$)

Worksheet 2

Ma 2, Level 4
Number and algebra
Test 6 Series 1

Dividing numbers up to 100 by single-digit numbers

Level Description element In solving number problems, pupils use a range of mental and written methods of computation with the four operations, including mental recall of multiplication facts up to 10×10.

Work out the answers to these 'division' calculations. Show the working.

1 $72 \div 9$ Answer (8)

2 $63 \div 7$ Answer (9)

3 $60 \div 2$ Answer (30)

4 $60 \div 3$ Answer (20)

5 $84 \div 2$ Answer (42)

6 $69 \div 3$ Answer (23)

7 $48 \div 3$ Answer (16)

8 $91 \div 7$ Answer (13)

9 $83 \div 6$ 13·83   Answer (or 13 r5 / or $13\frac{5}{6}$)

10 $67 \div 5$ 13·4   Answer (or 13 r2 / or $13\frac{2}{5}$)

Mathscheck | **Name** _____ **Date** _____

Ma 2, Level 4
Number and algebra
Test 7 Series 1

Adding decimals to two places
Level Description element [Pupils] add and subtract decimals to two places.

1 a
$$4.2 \\ +\,0.7 \over 4.9$$
b
$$4.6 \\ +\,0.5 \over 5.1$$
c
$$2.5 \\ +\,1.8 \over 4.3$$

2 a
$$3.5 \\ +\,9.6 \over 13.1$$
b
$$2.63 \\ +\,0.06 \over 2.69$$
c
$$5.17 \\ +\,0.08 \over 5.25$$

3 a
$$2.61 \\ +\,0.27 \over 2.88$$
b
$$6.54 \\ +\,0.36 \over 6.90$$
c
$$1.75 \\ +\,0.62 \over 2.37$$

4 a
$$4.79 \\ +\,0.65 \over 5.44$$
b
$$4.27 \\ +\,2.32 \over 6.59$$
c
$$3.46 \\ +\,6.28 \over 9.74$$

5 a
$$5.65 \\ +\,2.83 \over 8.48$$
b
$$3.96 \\ +\,2.85 \over 6.81$$
c
$$5.88 \\ +\,6.25 \over 12.13$$

Mathscheck | **Name** _____ **Date** _____

Ma 2, Level 4
Number and algebra
Test 7 Series 2

Adding decimals to two places
Level Description element [Pupils] add and subtract decimals to two places.

1 a
$$3.6 \\ +\,0.3 \over 3.9$$
b
$$5.8 \\ +\,0.8 \over 6.6$$
c
$$2.6 \\ +\,1.7 \over 4.3$$

2 a
$$5.8 \\ +\,6.5 \over 12.3$$
b
$$2.84 \\ +\,0.05 \over 2.89$$
c
$$3.48 \\ +\,0.06 \over 3.54$$

3 a
$$3.34 \\ +\,0.33 \over 3.67$$
b
$$7.29 \\ +\,0.28 \over 7.57$$
c
$$2.83 \\ +\,0.42 \over 3.25$$

4 a
$$3.97 \\ +\,0.56 \over 4.53$$
b
$$2.41 \\ +\,1.26 \over 3.67$$
c
$$3.28 \\ +\,6.46 \over 9.74$$

5 a
$$5.73 \\ +\,1.74 \over 7.47$$
b
$$4.85 \\ +\,1.96 \over 6.81$$
c
$$7.77 \\ +\,6.66 \over 14.43$$

Sheet 1 (Series 2)

Mathsheet

Ma 2, Level 4
Number and algebra
Test 8 Series 2

Name _____ *Date* _____

Subtracting decimals to two places
Level Description element [Pupils] add and subtract decimals to two places.

1 a
$$6 \cdot 7 - 3 \cdot 4 = 3 \cdot 3$$

b
$$8 \cdot 2 - 2 \cdot 7 = 5 \cdot 5$$

2 a
$$4 \cdot 59 - 0 \cdot 27 = 4 \cdot 32$$

b
$$6 \cdot 78 - 2 \cdot 63 = 4 \cdot 15$$

3 a
$$5 \cdot 55 - 0 \cdot 08 = 5 \cdot 47$$

b
$$3 \cdot 84 - 0 \cdot 59 = 3 \cdot 25$$

4 a
$$5 \cdot 73 - 2 \cdot 28 = 3 \cdot 45$$

b
$$4 \cdot 72 - 0 \cdot 91 = 3 \cdot 81$$

5 a
$$3 \cdot 68 - 1 \cdot 83 = 1 \cdot 85$$

b
$$5 \cdot 23 - 2 \cdot 78 = 2 \cdot 45$$

6 a
$$6 \cdot 20 - 1 \cdot 87 = 4 \cdot 33$$

b
$$7 \cdot 02 - 3 \cdot 84 = 3 \cdot 18$$

Sheet 2 (Series 1)

Mathsheet

Ma 2, Level 4
Number and algebra
Test 8 Series 1

Name _____ *Date* _____

Subtracting decimals to two places
Level Description element [Pupils] add and subtract decimals to two places.

1 a
$$5 \cdot 8 - 2 \cdot 6 = 3 \cdot 2$$

b
$$7 \cdot 3 - 3 \cdot 6 = 3 \cdot 7$$

2 a
$$3 \cdot 95 - 0 \cdot 72 = 3 \cdot 23$$

b
$$5 \cdot 92 - 2 \cdot 31 = 3 \cdot 61$$

3 a
$$4 \cdot 44 - 0 \cdot 07 = 4 \cdot 37$$

b
$$2 \cdot 72 - 0 \cdot 46 = 2 \cdot 26$$

4 a
$$6 \cdot 91 - 4 \cdot 79 = 2 \cdot 12$$

b
$$5 \cdot 58 - 0 \cdot 64 = 4 \cdot 94$$

5 a
$$4 \cdot 47 - 2 \cdot 62 = 1 \cdot 85$$

b
$$6 \cdot 15 - 2 \cdot 89 = 3 \cdot 26$$

6 a
$$7 \cdot 60 - 3 \cdot 78 = 3 \cdot 82$$

b
$$6 \cdot 07 - 1 \cdot 28 = 4 \cdot 79$$

Top worksheet

Ma 2, Level 4

Number and algebra
Test 9 Series 2

Rounding & approximating. Interpreting calculator displays

Level Description element In solving problems with or without a calculator, pupils check the reasonableness of their results by reference to their knowledge of the context or to the size of the numbers.

1 Round these numbers to the nearest 10.

a 73 → 70
b 395 → 400
c 26,599 → 26,600

2 Round these numbers to the nearest 100.

a 943 → 900
b 2650 → 2700
c 37,166 → 37,200

3 Round these numbers to the nearest 1000.

a 3678 → 4000
b 23,195 → 23,000
c 621,219 → 621,000

4 Round these numbers to the nearest whole number.

a 8·3 → 8
b 77·5 → 78
c 2391·6 → 2392

5 Choose and ring the 'best guess' of the answer to these calculations.

a 342 + 277   590   (620)   650   680
b 1722 + 3665   5000   5100   5200   (5400)
c 743 − 376   350   (370)   390   400
d 3500 − 578   2600   2700   2800   (2900)

6 A pad of 100 sheets of card is 2·4 cm thick.   *Use a calculator*

a 1 sheet has a thickness of (0·24) mm
b 225 sheets have a thickness of (5·4) cm

7 Write the missing numbers in these 'chains'.   *Use a calculator*

a 6 → −2·5 → =3·5 → ×3 → =10·5 → +9·9 → =20·4
b 5·3 → +2·6 → =7·9 → +0·2 → =8·1 → ÷·9 → =0·9
c 0·4 → ÷·4 → =1 → ×10 → +8·2 → =9·2

Bottom worksheet

Ma 2, Level 4

Number and algebra
Test 9 Series 1

Rounding & approximating. Interpreting calculator displays

Level Description element In solving problems with or without a calculator, pupils check the reasonableness of their results by reference to their knowledge of the context or to the size of the numbers.

1 Round these numbers to the nearest 10.

a 57 → 60
b 265 → 270
c 15,484 → 15,480

2 Round these numbers to the nearest 100.

a 629 → 600
b 1250 → 1300
c 26,257 → 26,300

3 Round these numbers to the nearest 1000.

a 1587 → 2000
b 17,246 → 17,000
c 121,712 → 122,000

4 Round these numbers to the nearest whole number.

a 6·4 → 6
b 95·6 → 96
c 1254·5 → 1255

5 Choose and ring the 'best guess' of the answer to these calculations.

a 236 + 381   550   600   (620)   650
b 2643 + 1989   4400   4500   (4600)   4700
c 621 − 187   370   400   (430)   460
d 2500 − 1678   600   700   (800)   900

6 A pad of 100 sheets of paper is 1·5 cm thick.   *Use a calculator*

a 1 sheet has a thickness of (0·15) mm
b 280 sheets have a thickness of (4·2) cm

7 Write the missing numbers in these 'chains'.   *Use a calculator*

a 4 → +3·3 → =7·3 → ×2 → =14·6 → −5·9 → =8·7
b 7·7 → ÷·7 → =1·1 → +7·9 → =9 → ÷·3 → =3
c 0·6 → ÷·3 → =0·2 → +9·8 → =10 → ÷·4 → =2·5

Mathcheck | **Name** | **Date**

Ma 2, Level 4
Number and algebra
Test 9 **Series 2**

Rounding & approximating. Interpreting calculator displays
Level Description element In solving problems with or without a calculator, pupils check the reasonableness of their results by reference to their knowledge of the context or to the size of the numbers.

8 Round each of the calculator displays to the **nearest whole number**.

a 6.78787 → ⑦
b 3.030303 → ③
c 0.9999 → ①
d 2.4455 → ②

9 Use a calculator. Write the calculator answer **and** round it to the **nearest whole number**.

	calculator	to the nearest whole number
a 37·19 + 48·93	86·12	86
b 81·77 − 18·88	62·89	63
c 9 × 0·77	6·93	7
d 92·5 ÷ 5	18·5	19

10 A family gets 7 newspapers each week, each costing 37p. The bill comes every 4 weeks. What is the total bill to the **nearest £1**? £ 10

11 What length of wood is left if four pieces measuring 1 m 37 cm, 2 m 98 cm, 77 cm and 3 m 50 cm are cut from a plank 10 metres long? (Answer in metres.) 1.38 m

12 Wire netting is sold **only** in full 1 metre lengths. How many metres must I buy to enclose this triangular rabbit run?

2 m 25 cm   2 m 25 cm
3 m 5 cm

8 m

© HarperCollins Publishers Ltd 1996

Mathcheck | **Name** | **Date**

Ma 2, Level 4
Number and algebra
Test 9 **Series 1**

Rounding & approximating. Interpreting calculator displays
Level Description element In solving problems with or without a calculator, pupils check the reasonableness of their results by reference to their knowledge of the context or to the size of the numbers.

8 Round each of the calculator displays to the **nearest whole number**.

a 3.14876 → ③
b 1.9090909 → ②
c 7.08088 → ⑦
d 0.77777 → ①

9 Use a calculator. Write the calculator answer **and** round it to the **nearest whole number**.

	calculator	to the nearest whole number
a 16·27 + 29·84	46·11	46
b 72·35 − 37·68	34·67	35
c 8 × 0·91	7·28	7
d 87·6 ÷ 4	21·9	22

10 A family gets 7 newspapers each week, each costing 42p. The bill comes every 4 weeks. What is the total bill to the **nearest £1**? £ 12

11 What length of wood is left if four pieces measuring 1 m 34 cm, 92 cm, 1 m 87 cm and 3 m are cut from a plank 10 metres long? (Answer in metres.) 2.87 m

12 Wire netting is sold **only** in full 1 metre lengths. How many metres must I buy to enclose this rectangular rabbit run?

88 cm   88 cm
1m 20 cm   1m 20 cm

5 m

© HarperCollins Publishers Ltd 1996

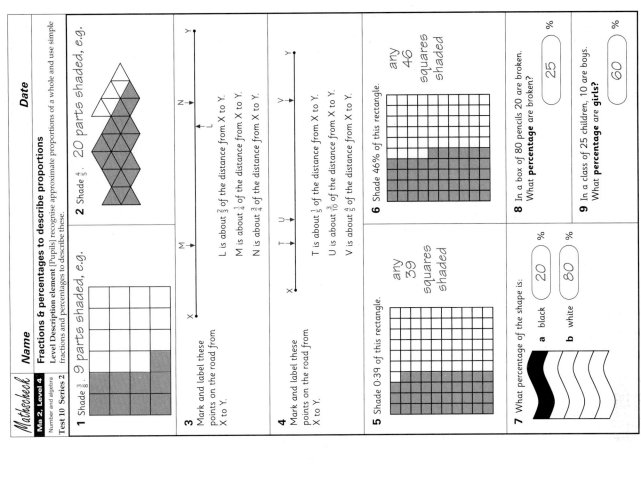

Ma 2, Level 4
Number and algebra
Test 10 Series 2

Fractions & percentages to describe proportions

Level Description element [Pupils] recognise approximate proportions of a whole and use simple fractions and percentages to describe these.

1 Shade $\frac{3}{8}$. *9 parts shaded, e.g.*

2 Shade $\frac{4}{5}$. *20 parts shaded, e.g.*

3 Mark and label these points on the road from X to Y.

X ——— M ——— N ——— Y

L is about $\frac{2}{3}$ of the distance from X to Y.
M is about $\frac{1}{4}$ of the distance from X to Y.
N is about $\frac{3}{4}$ of the distance from X to Y.

4 Mark and label these points on the road from X to Y.

X —— T U —— V —— Y

T is about $\frac{1}{5}$ of the distance from X to Y.
U is about $\frac{3}{10}$ of the distance from X to Y.
V is about $\frac{4}{5}$ of the distance from X to Y.

5 Shade 0·39 of this rectangle.

any 39 squares shaded

6 Shade 46% of this rectangle.

any 46 squares shaded

7 What percentage of the shape is:
  a black 20 %
  b white 80 %

8 In a box of 80 pencils 20 are broken.
What **percentage** are broken? 25 %

9 In a class of 25 children, 10 are boys.
What **percentage** are **girls?** 60 %

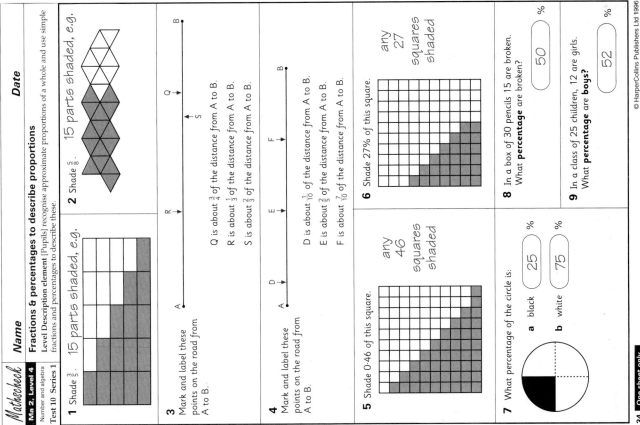

Ma 2, Level 4
Number and algebra
Test 10 Series 1

Fractions & percentages to describe proportions

Level Description element [Pupils] recognise approximate proportions of a whole and use simple fractions and percentages to describe these.

1 Shade $\frac{3}{5}$. *15 parts shaded, e.g.*

2 Shade $\frac{5}{8}$. *15 parts shaded, e.g.*

3 Mark and label these points on the road from A to B.

A ——— R S —— Q ——— B

Q is about $\frac{3}{4}$ of the distance from A to B.
R is about $\frac{1}{3}$ of the distance from A to B.
S is about $\frac{2}{3}$ of the distance from A to B.

4 Mark and label these points on the road from A to B.

A D —— E —— F ——— B

D is about $\frac{1}{10}$ of the distance from A to B.
E is about $\frac{2}{5}$ of the distance from A to B.
F is about $\frac{7}{10}$ of the distance from A to B.

5 Shade 0·46 of this square.

any 46 squares shaded

6 Shade 27% of this square.

any 27 squares shaded

7 What percentage of the circle is:
  a black 25 %
  b white 75 %

8 In a box of 30 pencils 15 are broken.
What **percentage** are broken? 50 %

9 In a class of 25 children, 12 are girls.
What **percentage** are **boys?** 52 %

Left worksheet (Series 1)

Mathsheek **Name** **Date**

Ma 2, Level 4
Number and algebra
Test 11 Series 1

Number patterns & related terminology
Level Description element Pupils explore and describe number patterns, and relationships
including multiple, factor and square.

1 In this set of numbers a line of
four has been ringed.

2	3	4	5	6
12	13	14	15	16
22	23	24	25	26
32	33	34	35	36
42	43	44	45	46

Explain why they make a
number pattern.

Various answers, e.g.

- *add/subtract 9*

- *tens sequence
  of 1, 2, 3, 4*

- *units sequence
  of 6, 5, 4, 3*

- *digital sum of 7 for
  each number*

2 Look carefully at this set of
numbers.

2	6	10	14	18
4	12	20	28	36
6	18	30	42	54
8	24	40	56	72
10	30	50	70	90

Ring four numbers in a line
which make a pattern.

Explain why they make a
number pattern.

Various answers, e.g.

- *addition/
  subtraction*
- *tens digit
  sequence*
- *units digit
  sequence*
- *digital sums*

First of three sheets 35

Right worksheet (Series 2)

Mathsheek **Name** **Date**

Ma 2, Level 4
Number and algebra
Test 11 Series 2

Number patterns & related terminology
Level Description element Pupils explore and describe number patterns, and relationships
including multiple, factor and square.

1 In this set of numbers a line of
four has been ringed.

2	3	4	5	6
12	13	14	15	16
22	23	24	25	26
32	33	34	35	36
42	43	44	45	46

Explain why they make a
number pattern.

Various answers, e.g.

- *add/subtract 9*

- *tens sequence of
  0, 1, 2, 3*

- *units sequence of
  5, 4, 3, 2*

- *digital sum of 5
  for each number*

2 Look carefully at this set of
numbers.

4	8	12	16	20
8	16	24	32	40
12	24	36	48	60
16	32	48	64	80
20	40	60	80	100

Ring four numbers in a line
which make a pattern.

Explain why they make a
number pattern.

Various answers, e.g.

- *addition/
  subtraction*
- *tens digit
  sequence*
- *units digit
  sequence*
- *digital sums*

First of three sheets 69

Ma 2, Level 4

Number and algebra
Test 11 **Series 1**

Number patterns & related terminology

Level Description element Pupils explore and describe number patterns, and relationships including multiple, factor and square.

3 Look at these patterns of matchsticks.

5 matchsticks

9 matchsticks

13 matchsticks

a Draw the next pattern.

b Write the next number.

17

c Write sentences about the patterns of shapes and numbers.
Various answers, e.g.

● *building on the previous pattern*

● *adding 4 matches each time*

● *fifth pattern contains 21*

4 Complete these 'doubling and halving' patterns.

a $1 \times 72 = 2 \times$ 36 $= 4 \times$ 18 $= 8 \times$ 9

b $3 \times 32 = 6 \times$ 16 $= 12 \times$ 8 $= 24 \times$ 4

5 If $13 \times 23 = 299$ which three of these number statements are true? (Tick your choices.)

a $23 + 13 = 299$

b $299 \div 13 = 23$ ✓

c $299 \div 23 = 13$ ✓

d $299 - 23 = 13$

e $23 \times 13 = 299$ ✓

Ma 2, Level 4

Number and algebra
Test 11 **Series 2**

Number patterns & related terminology

Level Description element Pupils explore and describe number patterns, and relationships including multiple, factor and square.

3 Look at these patterns of matchsticks.

3 matchsticks

5 matchsticks

7 matchsticks

a Draw the next pattern.

b Write the next number.

9

c Write sentences about the patterns of shapes and numbers.
Various answers, e.g.

● *building on the previous pattern*

● *adding two matches each time*

● *fifth pattern contains 11*

4 Complete these 'doubling and halving' patterns.

a $1 \times 48 = 2 \times$ 24 $= 4 \times$ 12 $= 8 \times$ 6

b $3 \times 36 = 6 \times$ 18 $= 12 \times$ 9

5 If $14 \times 24 = 336$ which three of these number statements are true? (Tick your choices.)

a $336 \div 14 = 24$ ✓

b $14 + 24 = 336$

c $24 \times 14 = 336$ ✓

d $336 \div 24 = 14$ ✓

e $24 \div 14 = 336$

Series 2 (Sheet — page 71)

Ma 2, Level 4
Number and algebra
Test 11 Series 2

Name _____ **Date** _____

Number patterns & related terminology
Level Description element Pupils explore and describe number patterns, and relationships including multiple, factor and square.

Write the missing numbers.

6 1, 3, 5, 7, (9), 11

7 5, 10, 15, (20), (25), 30

8 20, 16, 12, (8), (4), 0

9 403, 402, 401, (400), (399)

10 52, 49, 46, (43), (40)

11 80, 40, (20), 10, (5)

12 3, 6, 12, 24, (48), (96)

13 2, 4, 7, 11, (16), (22)

14 Look at these numbers.

18   8   30   40   45   90

Write those which are:

a multiples of 2 — (8) 18 (30) (40) (90)

b multiples of 10 — (30) (40) (90)

c multiples of 5 — (30) (45) (90)

d multiples of 2 **and** 5 — (30) (40) (90)

e multiples of 2 **and** 10 — (30) (40) (90)

15 Complete this statement:
The **factors** of 36 are 1, 2, 3, 4, 6, 9, 12, 18, 36

Series 1 (Sheet — page 37)

Ma 2, Level 4
Number and algebra
Test 11 Series 1

Name _____ **Date** _____

Number patterns & related terminology
Level Description element Pupils explore and describe number patterns, and relationships including multiple, factor and square.

Write the missing numbers.

6 2, 4, 6, 8, (10), (12)

7 3, 6, 9, (12), (15), 18

8 25, 20, 15, (10), (5), 0

9 596, 597, 598, (599), (600)

10 40, 37, 34, (31), (28)

11 160, 80, 40, (20), (10)

12 1, 2, 4, 8, 16, (32), (64)

13 1, 3, 6, 10, (15), (21)

14 Look at these numbers.

27   45   80   28   10   30   6

Write those which are:

a multiples of 2 — (6) (10) (28) (30) (80)

b multiples of 10 — (10) (30) (80)

c multiples of 5 — (10) (30) (45) (80)

d multiples of 2 **and** 5 — (10) (30) (80)

e multiples of 2 **and** 10 — (10) (30) (80)

15 Complete this statement:
The **factors** of 24 are 1, 2, 3, 4, 6, 8, 12, 24

Mathscheck — Name — Date

Ma 2, Level 4
Number and algebra
Test 12 Series 2

Using simple formulae expressed in words

Level Description element [Pupils] have begun to use simple formulae expressed in words.

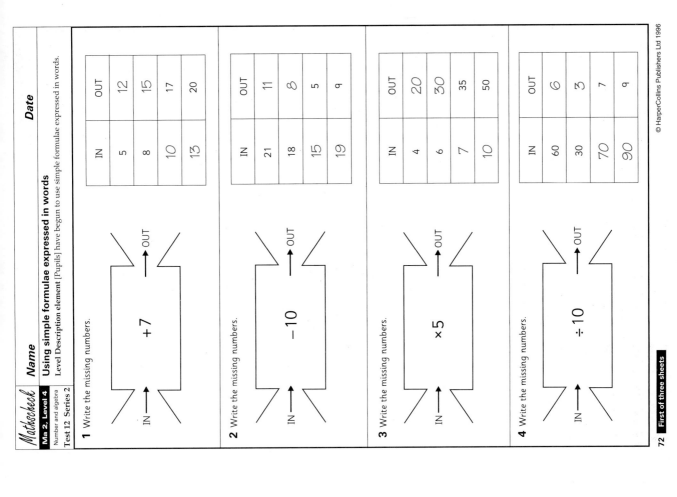

1 Write the missing numbers. $+7$

IN	OUT
5	12
8	15
10	17
13	20

2 Write the missing numbers. -10

IN	OUT
21	11
18	8
15	5
19	9

3 Write the missing numbers. $\times 5$

IN	OUT
4	20
6	30
7	35
10	50

4 Write the missing numbers. $\div 10$

IN	OUT
60	6
30	3
70	7
90	9

Mathscheck — Name — Date

Ma 2, Level 4
Number and algebra
Test 12 Series 1

Using simple formulae expressed in words

Level Description element [Pupils] have begun to use simple formulae expressed in words.

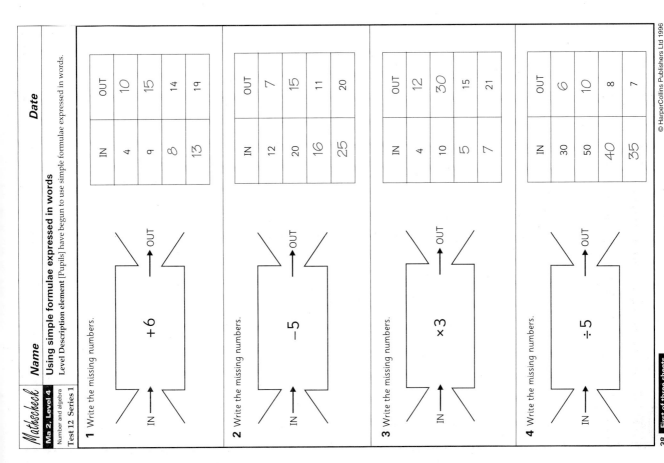

1 Write the missing numbers. $+6$

IN	OUT
4	10
9	15
8	14
13	19

2 Write the missing numbers. -5

IN	OUT
12	7
20	15
16	11
25	20

3 Write the missing numbers. $\times 3$

IN	OUT
4	12
10	30
5	15
7	21

4 Write the missing numbers. $\div 5$

IN	OUT
30	6
50	10
40	8
35	7

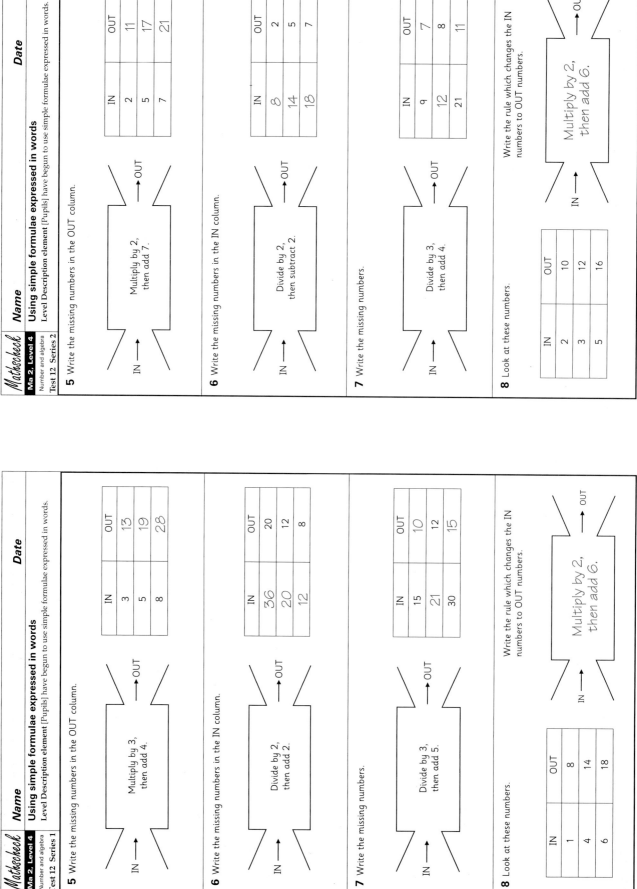

Mathscheck | **Name** | **Date**

Ma 2, Level 4
Number and algebra
Test 12 Series 2

Using simple formulae expressed in words

Level Description element [Pupils] have begun to use simple formulae expressed in words.

5 Write the missing numbers in the OUT column.

IN → [Multiply by 2, then add 7.] → OUT

IN	OUT
2	11
5	17
7	21

6 Write the missing numbers in the IN column.

IN → [Divide by 2, then subtract 2.] → OUT

IN	OUT
8	2
14	5
18	7

7 Write the missing numbers.

IN → [Divide by 3, then add 4.] → OUT

IN	OUT
9	7
12	8
21	11

8 Look at these numbers.

IN	OUT
2	10
3	12
5	16

Write the rule which changes the IN numbers to OUT numbers.

IN → [Multiply by 2, then add 6.] → OUT

Mathscheck | **Name** | **Date**

Ma 2, Level 4
Number and algebra
Test 12 Series 1

Using simple formulae expressed in words

Level Description element [Pupils] have begun to use simple formulae expressed in words.

5 Write the missing numbers in the OUT column.

IN → [Multiply by 3, then add 4.] → OUT

IN	OUT
3	13
5	19
8	28

6 Write the missing numbers in the IN column.

IN → [Divide by 2, then add 2.] → OUT

IN	OUT
36	20
20	12
12	8

7 Write the missing numbers.

IN → [Divide by 3, then add 5.] → OUT

IN	OUT
15	10
21	12
30	15

8 Look at these numbers.

IN	OUT
1	8
4	14
6	18

Write the rule which changes the IN numbers to OUT numbers.

IN → [Multiply by 2, then add 6.] → OUT

Top sheet

Mathscheck | **Name** | **Date**

Using simple formulae expressed in words
Level Description element [Pupils] have begun to use simple formulae expressed in words.

9 I add 2 to a number, then multiply the result by 5. The answer is 30.
What number did I start with?

I started with (4)

10 I halve a number, then add 2 and the result is 16.
What is the number I started with?

I started with (28)

11 Write the missing number.

double then
subtract 1

4 → 7
5 → 9
6 → 11

12 Write the missing number.

halve then
subtract 1

4 → 1
14 → 6
24 → 11

13 Complete the rule.

Week	1	2	3	4	5	6
Total amount saved		20 p	40 p	60 p	80 p	£1	£1·20

Rule:
Total amount saved = number of (weeks) × (20) p

14 Complete the rule.

Jen's age	4	5	6	7	8	9
Ali's age	7	8	9	10	11	12

Rule:
Jen's age = [Ali] 's age − (3)

Bottom sheet

Mathscheck | **Name** | **Date**

Using simple formulae expressed in words
Level Description element [Pupils] have begun to use simple formulae expressed in words.

9 I add 5 to a number, then multiply the result by 2. The answer is 16.
What number did I start with?

I started with (3)

10 I double a number, then add 3 and the result is 29.
What is the number I started with?

I started with (13)

11 Write the missing number.

double then
add 1

6 → 13
8 → 17
10 → 21

12 Write the missing number.

halve then
add 1

8 → 5
10 → 6
22 → 12

13 Complete the rule.

Week	1	2	3	4	5	6
Total pocket money	£1	£2	£3	£4	£5	£6

Rule:
Total pocket money = £ (1) × number of (weeks)

14 Complete the rule.

Jane's age	6	7	8	9	10	11
Karim's age	1	2	3	4	5	6

Rule:
Jane's age = [Karim] 's age + (5)

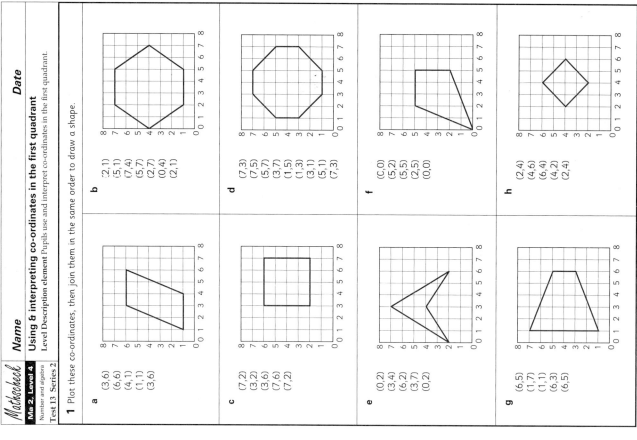

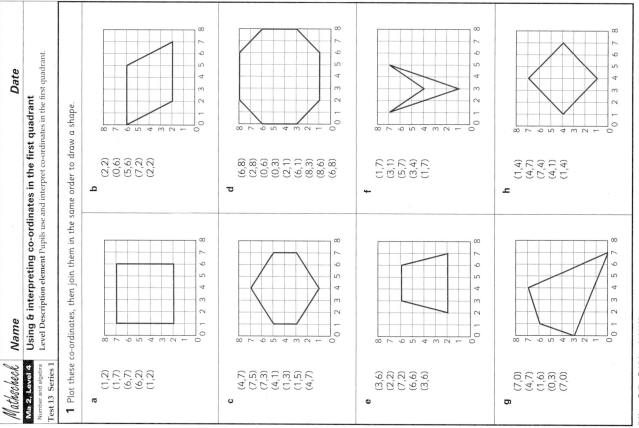

Ma 2, Level 4
Number and algebra
Test 13 Series 2

Using & interpreting co-ordinates in the first quadrant

Level Description element Pupils use and interpret co-ordinates in the first quadrant.

1 Plot these co-ordinates, then join them in the same order to draw a shape.

a (3,6) (6,6) (4,1) (1,1) (3,6)

b (2,1) (5,1) (7,4) (5,7) (2,7) (0,4) (2,1)

c (7,2) (3,2) (3,6) (7,6) (7,2)

d (7,3) (7,5) (5,7) (3,7) (1,5) (1,3) (3,1) (5,1) (7,3)

e (0,2) (3,4) (6,2) (3,7) (0,2)

f (C,0) (5,2) (5,5) (2,5) (0,0)

g (6,5) (1,7) (1,1) (6,3) (6,5)

h (2,4) (4,6) (6,4) (4,2) (2,4)

Ma 2, Level 4
Number and algebra
Test 13 Series 1

Using & interpreting co-ordinates in the first quadrant

Level Description element Pupils use and interpret co-ordinates in the first quadrant.

1 Plot these co-ordinates, then join them in the same order to draw a shape.

a (1,2) (1,7) (6,7) (6,2) (1,2)

b (2,2) (0,6) (5,6) (7,2) (2,2)

c (4,7) (7,5) (7,3) (4,1) (1,3) (1,5) (4,7)

d (6,8) (2,8) (0,6) (0,3) (2,1) (6,1) (8,3) (8,6) (6,8)

e (3,6) (2,2) (7,2) (6,6) (3,6)

f (1,7) (3,1) (5,7) (3,4) (1,7)

g (7,0) (4,7) (1,6) (0,3) (7,0)

h (1,4) (4,7) (7,4) (4,1) (1,4)

Constructing simple 3-D models from nets

Ma 3, Level 4
Shape, space and measures
Test 14 Series 2

Level Description element Pupils make 3-D mathematical models by linking given faces or edges, draw common 2-D shapes in different orientations on grids, and identify congruent shapes and orders of rotational symmetry.

1 Use centimetre squared paper, scissors, ruler, pencil and glue.
a On the squared paper, draw the **nets** to make each shape.
b Construct the 3-D shape from the net, full size.

Look carefully at the measurements!

The 3-D shapes are constructed to an appropriate degree of accuracy.

A cube 6 cm 6 cm 6 cm

B cuboid 5 cm 6 cm 4 cm

C prism 4 cm 4 cm 4 cm 4 cm 8 cm

D pyramid 6 cm 6 cm 6 cm

Constructing simple 3-D models from nets

Ma 3, Level 4
Shape, space and measures
Test 14 Series 1

Level Description element Pupils make 3-D mathematical models by linking given faces or edges, draw common 2-D shapes in different orientations on grids, and identify congruent shapes and orders of rotational symmetry.

1 Use centimetre squared paper, scissors, ruler, pencil and glue.
a On the squared paper, draw the **nets** to make each shape.
b Construct the 3-D shape from the net, full size.

Look carefully at the measurements!

The 3-D shapes are constructed to an appropriate degree of accuracy.

A cube 5 cm 5 cm 5 cm

B cuboid 4 cm 5 cm 3 cm

C prism 5 cm 5 cm 5 cm 10 cm

D pyramid 5 cm 5 cm 5 cm

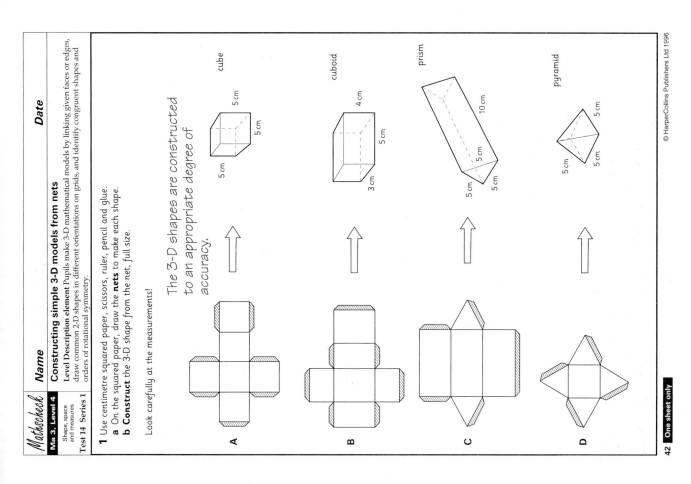

111

Top sheet (Series 2)

Ma 3. Level 4

Shape, space and measures

Test 15 Series 2

Constructing 2-D shapes & identifying congruence

Level Description element Pupils make 3-D mathematical models by linking given faces or edges, draw common 2-D shapes in different orientations on grids, and identify congruent shapes and orders of rotational symmetry.

You need: compasses, ruler, sharp pencil, set square.

1 Join the angle to the correct name.

(right angle) (reflex angle) (acute angle) (obtuse angle)

2 Draw a line which is **parallel** to the line PQ.

P

Q

Other positions are possible.

3 Draw a **diagonal** on this shape.

Or the alternative diagonals

4 Draw a line from X, which is **perpendicular** to the line AB.

A

X

B

5 a Draw a **square** of side 3·5 cm.

b Mark its **centre** with a cross and label it M.

Other positions of the square are possible.

M

6 a Draw a **rectangle** measuring 7·5 cm by 4·5 cm.

b Mark its **centre** with a cross and label it M.

Other positions of the rectangle are possible.

M

Bottom sheet (Series 1)

Ma 3. Level 4

Shape, space and measures

Test 15 Series 1

Constructing 2-D shapes & identifying congruence

Level Description element Pupils make 3-D mathematical models by linking given faces or edges, draw common 2-D shapes in different orientations on grids, and identify congruent shapes and orders of rotational symmetry.

You need: compasses, ruler, sharp pencil, set square.

1 Join the angle to the correct name.

(acute angle) (right angle) (reflex angle) (obtuse angle)

2 Draw a line which is **parallel** to the line AB.

A

B

Other positions are possible.

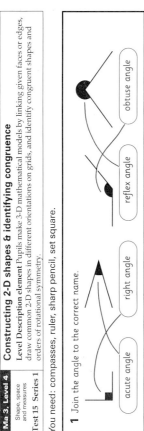

3 Draw a **diagonal** on this shape.

Or the alternative diagonal

4 Draw a line from P, which is **perpendicular** to the line XY.

Y

P

X

5 a Draw a **square** of side 4·5 cm.

b Mark its **centre** with a clear 'dot' and label it C.

Other positions of the square are possible.

C

6 a Draw a **rectangle** measuring 8½ cm by 3½ cm.

b Mark its **centre** with a clear 'dot' and label it C.

Other positions of the rectangle are possible.

C

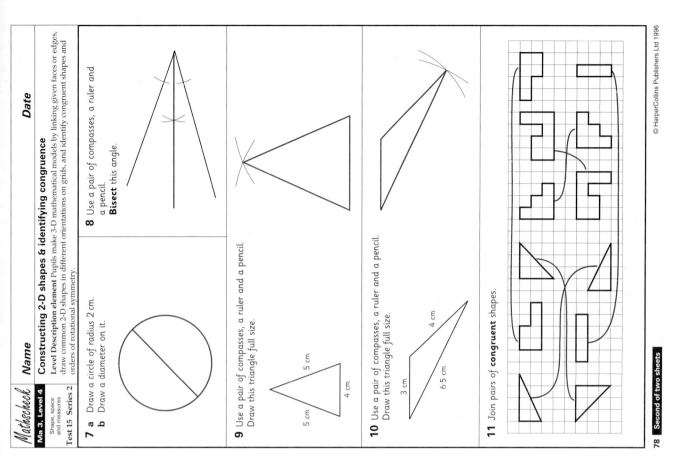

Ma 3, Level 4

Shape, space and measures

Test 15 Series 2

Constructing 2-D shapes & identifying congruence

Level Description element Pupils make 3-D mathematical models by linking given faces or edges, draw common 2-D shapes in different orientations on grids, and identify congruent shapes and orders of rotational symmetry.

7 a Draw a circle of radius 2 cm.
b Draw a diameter on it.

8 Use a pair of compasses, a ruler and a pencil.
Bisect this angle.

9 Use a pair of compasses, a ruler and a pencil.
Draw this triangle full size.

5 cm
5 cm
4 cm

10 Use a pair of compasses, a ruler and a pencil.
Draw this triangle full size.

3 cm
4 cm
6·5 cm

11 Join pairs of **congruent** shapes.

© HarperCollins Publishers Ltd 1996

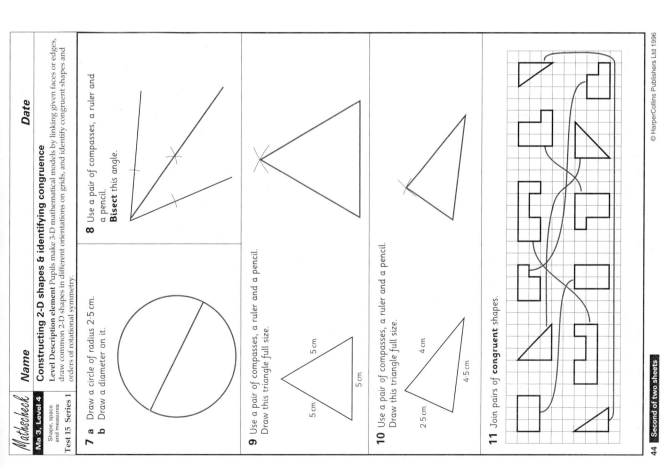

Ma 3, Level 4

Shape, space and measures

Test 15 Series 1

Constructing 2-D shapes & identifying congruence

Level Description element Pupils make 3-D mathematical models by linking given faces or edges, draw common 2-D shapes in different orientations on grids, and identify congruent shapes and orders of rotational symmetry.

7 a Draw a circle of radius 2·5 cm.
b Draw a diameter on it.

8 Use a pair of compasses, a ruler and a pencil.
Bisect this angle.

9 Use a pair of compasses, a ruler and a pencil.
Draw this triangle full size.

5 cm
5 cm
5 cm

10 Use a pair of compasses, a ruler and a pencil.
Draw this triangle full size.

2·5 cm
4 cm
4·5 cm

11 Join pairs of **congruent** shapes.

© HarperCollins Publishers Ltd 1996

113

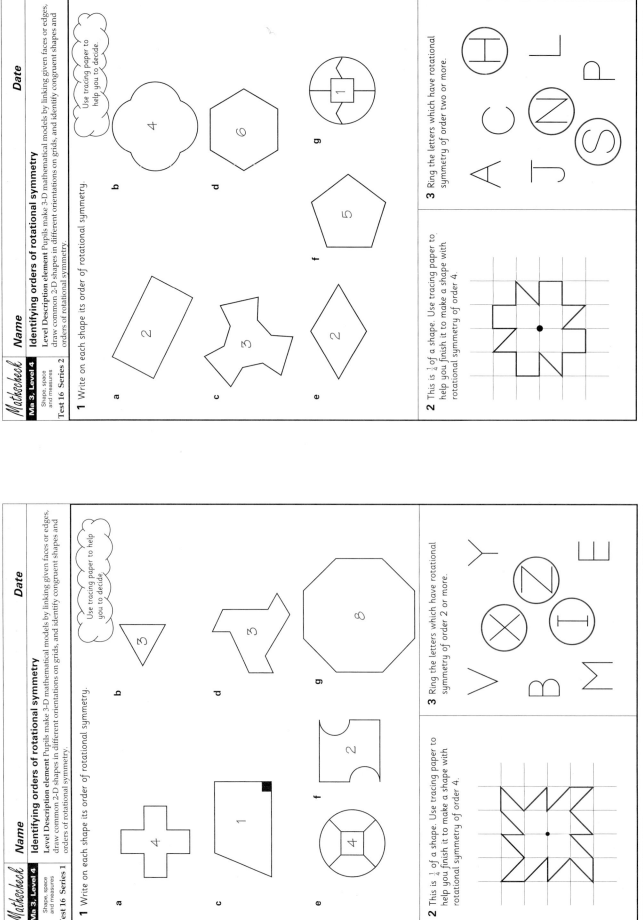

Page 1 (page 114)

Ma 3, Level 4
Shape, space and measures
Test 16 Series 1

Identifying orders of rotational symmetry

Level Description element Pupils make 3-D mathematical models by linking given faces or edges, draw common 2-D shapes in different orientations on grids, and identify congruent shapes and orders of rotational symmetry.

1 Write on each shape its order of rotational symmetry.

Use tracing paper to help you to decide.

a 4

b 3

c 1

d 3

e 4

f 2

g 8

2 This is $\frac{1}{4}$ of a shape. Use tracing paper to help you finish it to make a shape with rotational symmetry of order 4.

3 Ring the letters which have rotational symmetry of order 2 or more.

V X Y B Z I M O E

Page 2 (page 79)

Ma 3, Level 4
Shape, space and measures
Test 16 Series 2

Identifying orders of rotational symmetry

Level Description element Pupils make 3-D mathematical models by linking given faces or edges, draw common 2-D shapes in different orientations on grids, and identify congruent shapes and orders of rotational symmetry.

1 Write on each shape its order of rotational symmetry.

Use tracing paper to help you to decide.

a 2

b 4

c 3

d 6

e 2

f 5

g 1

2 This is $\frac{1}{4}$ of a shape. Use tracing paper to help you finish it to make a shape with rotational symmetry of order 4.

3 Ring the letters which have rotational symmetry of order two or more.

A C H J N L S P

118

Ma 3, Level 4

Reflecting simple shapes in a mirror line

Shape, space and measures

Level Description element [Pupils] reflect simple shapes in a mirror line.

Test 17 Series 2

1 Reflect the designs in the mirror lines to show 2-D symmetrical shapes.

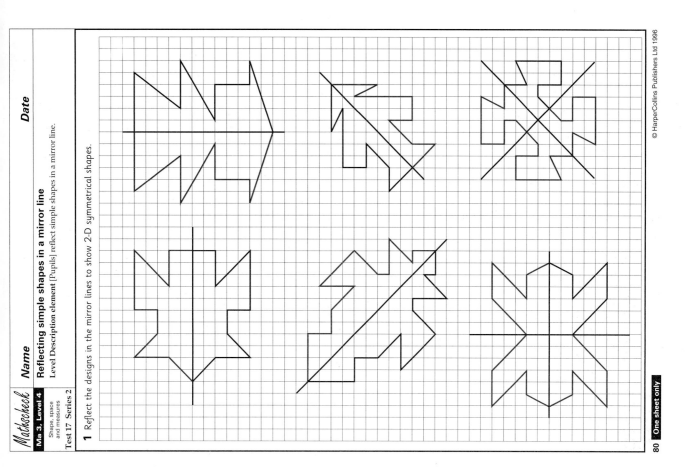

Ma 3, Level 4

Reflecting simple shapes in a mirror line

Shape, space and measures

Level Description element [Pupils] reflect simple shapes in a mirror line.

Test 17 Series 1

1 Reflect the designs in the mirror lines to show 2-D symmetrical shapes.

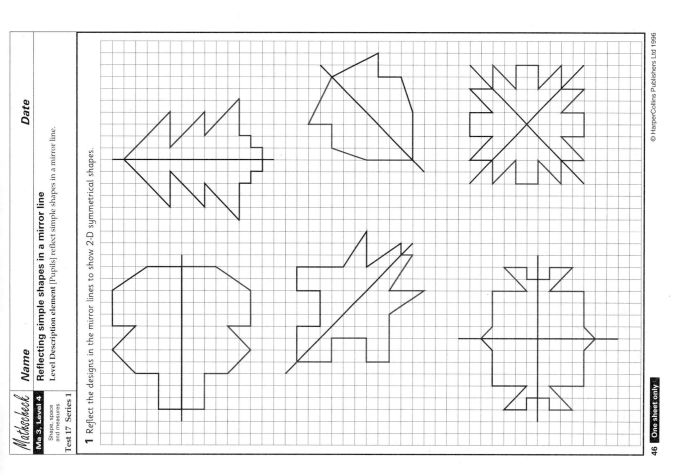

Top worksheet

Mathscheck | **Name** | **Date**

Ma 3. Level 4
Shape, space and measures
Test 18 Series 2

Interpreting numbers on measuring instruments

Level Description element [Pupils] choose and use appropriate units and instruments, interpreting, with appropriate accuracy, numbers on a range of measuring instruments.

1 This scale represents a distance of 2 metres.

Write in **decimal form** the measurement from A shown by the arrows.

X is (1·35) metres from A.   Y is (1·77) metres from A.

2 Write the times shown in digital form.

a (6·11)   b (2·36)

3 Write the weights shown on the scales.

a (810 g)   b (590 g)

4 Write the the amount of liquid in each container.

a (190 ml)   b (330 ml)

5 Write the size of these angles.

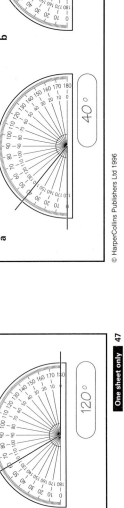

a (40°)   b (110°)

One sheet only 81

Bottom worksheet

Mathscheck | **Name** | **Date**

Ma 3. Level 4
Shape, space and measures
Test 18 Series 1

Interpreting numbers on measuring instruments

Level Description element [Pupils] choose and use appropriate units and instruments, interpreting, with appropriate accuracy, numbers on a range of measuring instruments.

1 This scale represents a distance of 2 metres.

Write in **decimal form** the measurement from A shown by the arrows.

P is (1·37) metres from A.   Q is (1·93) metres from A.

2 Write the times shown in digital form.

a (8·21)   b (3·48)

3 Write the weights shown on the scales.

a (890 g)   b (610 g)

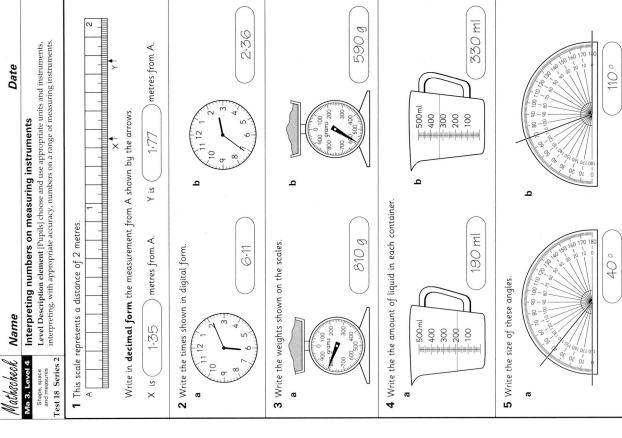

4 Write the the amount of liquid in each container.

a (270 ml)   b (420 ml)

5 Write the size of these angles.

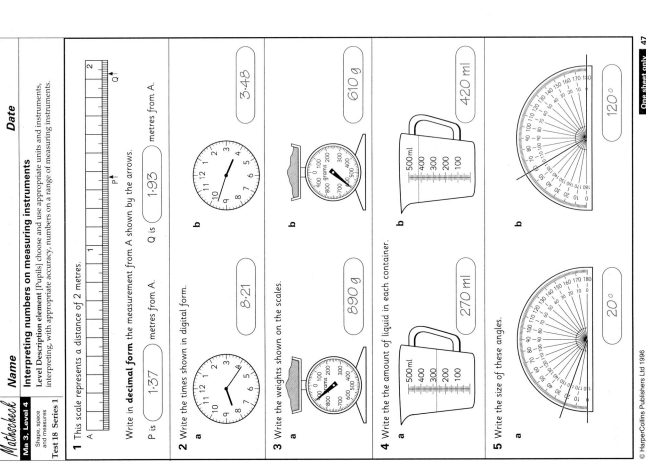

a (20°)   b (120°)

One sheet only 47

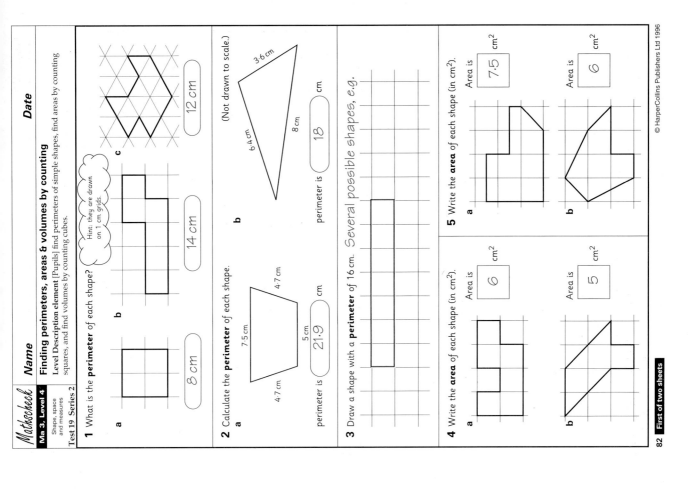

Mathscheck **Name** _____ **Date** _____

Ma 3, Level 4
Shape, space and measures
Test 19 Series 2

Finding perimeters, areas & volumes by counting

Level Description element [Pupils] find perimeters of simple shapes, find areas by counting squares, and find volumes by counting cubes.

1 What is the **perimeter** of each shape?

Hint: they are drawn on 1 cm grids.

a (8 cm) b (14 cm) c (12 cm)

2 Calculate the **perimeter** of each shape. (Not drawn to scale.)

a 4·7 cm 7·5 cm 4·7 cm 5 cm   perimeter is (21·9) cm

b 3·6 cm 6·4 cm 8 cm   perimeter is (18) cm

3 Draw a shape with a **perimeter** of 16 cm. *Several possible shapes, e.g.*

4 Write the **area** of each shape (in cm²).

a Area is (6) cm²

b Area is (5) cm²

5 Write the **area** of each shape (in cm²).

a Area is (7·5) cm²

b Area is (6) cm²

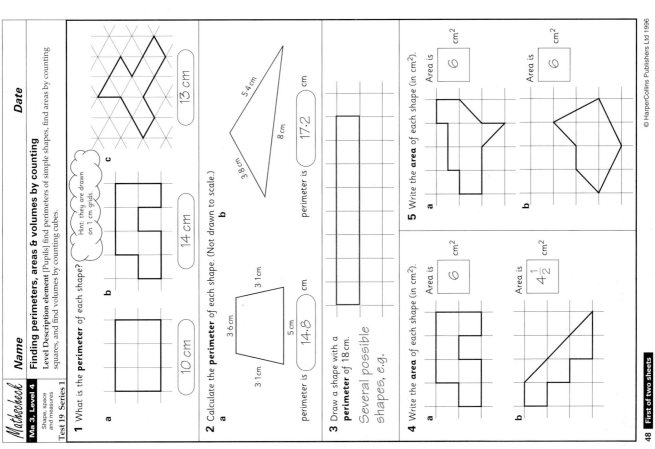

Mathscheck **Name** _____ **Date** _____

Ma 3, Level 4
Shape, space and measures
Test 19 Series 1

Finding perimeters, areas & volumes by counting

Level Description element [Pupils] find perimeters of simple shapes, find areas by counting squares, and find volumes by counting cubes.

1 What is the **perimeter** of each shape?

Hint: they are drawn on 1 cm grids.

a (10 cm) b (14 cm) c (13 cm)

2 Calculate the **perimeter** of each shape. (Not drawn to scale.)

a 3·6 cm 3·1 cm 3·1 cm 5 cm   perimeter is (14·8) cm

b 5·4 cm 3·8 cm 8 cm   perimeter is (17·2) cm

3 Draw a shape with a **perimeter** of 18 cm. *Several possible shapes, e.g.*

4 Write the **area** of each shape (in cm²).

a Area is (6) cm²

b Area is (4½) cm²

5 Write the **area** of each shape (in cm²).

a Area is (6) cm²

b Area is (6) cm²

Ma 3, Level 4

Shape, space and measures

Test 19 Series 2

Finding perimeters, areas & volumes by counting

Level Description element [Pupils] find perimeters of simple shapes, find areas by counting squares, and find volumes by counting cubes.

6 Find the approximate **area** of this shape (in cm²).

Approximate area is [9] cm²

7 Draw a shape with an **area** of 9½ cm².

Several shapes are possible, e.g.

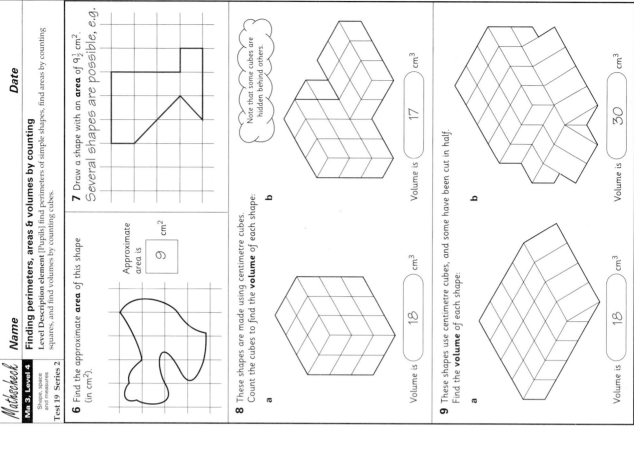

8 These shapes are made using centimetre cubes. Count the cubes to find the **volume** of each shape:

Note that some cubes are hidden behind others.

a

Volume is [18] cm³

b

Volume is [17] cm³

9 These shapes use centimetre cubes, and some have been cut in half. Find the **volume** of each shape:

a

Volume is [18] cm³

b

Volume is [30] cm³

Ma 3, Level 4

Shape, space and measures

Test 19 Series 1

Finding perimeters, areas & volumes by counting

Level Description element [Pupils] find perimeters of simple shapes, find areas by counting squares, and find volumes by counting cubes.

6 Find the approximate **area** of this shape (in cm²).

Approximate area is [9] cm²

7 Draw a shape with an **area** of 7½ cm².

Several shapes are possible, e.g.

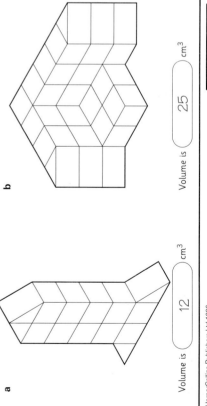

8 These shapes are made using centimetre cubes. Count the cubes to find the **volume** of each shape.

Note that some cubes are hidden behind others.

a

Volume is [24] cm³

b

Volume is [20] cm³

9 These shapes use centimetre cubes, and some have been cut in half. Find the **volume** of each shape.

a

Volume is [12] cm³

b

Volume is [25] cm³

Ma 4, Level 4   **Collecting & recording data**

Handling data   Level Description element Pupils collect discrete data and record them using a frequency table.

Test 20   Series 2

1 Choose a topic for which data would have to be collected. Write its title here.

Responses depend on the pupil's choice of topic.

2 Use this grid to help you draw a tally chart or frequency table. Use your chart or table to record your data.

Responses depend on the pupil's choice of topic.

3 Draw a chart or graph of your data on this grid.

Responses depend on the pupil's choice of topic.

Mathscheck   **Name**   *Date*

Ma 4, Level 4   **Collecting & recording data**

Handling data   Level Description element Pupils collect discrete data and record them using a frequency table.

Test 20   Series 1

1 Choose a topic for which data would have to be collected. Write its title here.

Responses depend on the pupil's choice of topic.

2 Use this grid to help you draw a tally chart or frequency table. Use your chart or table to record your data.

Responses depend on the pupil's choice of topic.

3 Draw a chart or graph of your data on this grid.

Responses depend on the pupil's choice of topic.

50   **One sheet only**

© HarperCollins Publishers Ltd 1996

Series 2 (page 85)

Recognising & using the mode & median
Level Description element [Pupils] understand and use the mode and median.

1 Write the **mode** of each set of numbers.

a   5   4   5   6   5   5   6   Mode is (5)

b   9   5   9   7   9   6   5   9   9   5   Mode is (9)

c   7.5   8.1   8.2   7.5   8.2   7.5   Mode is (7.5)

2 Write the **median** of each set of numbers.

a   7   6   7   6   8   Median is (7)

b   6   6   7   7   7   8   Median is (7)

c   2.31   2.40   2.25   2.34   2.51   2.29   2.36   Median is (2.34)

3 This table shows the shoe sizes of 30 children in a class.

Leroy	5	Helen	$3\frac{1}{2}$	Moshe	$4\frac{1}{2}$
Mary	$5\frac{1}{2}$	Tom	$4\frac{1}{2}$	Miriam	5
Marlene	7	Sarah	$6\frac{1}{2}$	Norma	$4\frac{1}{2}$
Alan	5	Indira	1	Cyril	$4\frac{1}{2}$
Ali	$4\frac{1}{2}$	Jean	$3\frac{1}{2}$	Azil	$5\frac{1}{2}$
Diane	$2\frac{1}{2}$	Lucy	2	Jafar	$3\frac{1}{2}$
Ewen	6	Justin	4	Lisa	$6\frac{1}{2}$
Colin	$4\frac{1}{2}$	Danielle	$4\frac{1}{2}$	Katy	$4\frac{1}{2}$
Penny	4	Peter	3	Tarun	4
Pablo	3	Fatima	$1\frac{1}{2}$	Rajindar	2

a Complete this table of the shoe sizes.

Shoe size	1	$1\frac{1}{2}$	2	$2\frac{1}{2}$	3	$3\frac{1}{2}$	4	$4\frac{1}{2}$	5	$5\frac{1}{2}$	6	$6\frac{1}{2}$	7
Number of children	1	1	2	1	2	3	3	8	3	2	1	2	1

b The median shoe size is ($4\frac{1}{2}$)

c The modal shoe size is ($4\frac{1}{2}$)

Series 1 (page 51)

Recognising & using the mode & median
Level Description element [Pupils] understand and use the mode and median.

1 Write the **mode** of each set of numbers.

a   8   7   8   7   6   7   Mode is (7)

b   7   3   7   5   7   4   3   7   7   3   Mode is (7)

c   8.5   9.2   8.5   9.2   8.5   9.1   9.2   8.5   Mode is (8.5)

2 Write the **median** of each set of numbers.

a   4   3   4   3   5   Median is (4)

b   9   9   10   10   10   11   Median is (10)

c   1.36   1.29   1.51   1.34   1.25   1.40   1.31   Median is (1.34)

3 This table shows the shoe sizes of 30 children in a class.

Kamaljit	$4\frac{1}{2}$	Paul	4	Hayley	6
Laura	1	Tony	$3\frac{1}{2}$	Harpreet	$6\frac{1}{2}$
Monica	$3\frac{1}{2}$	Charlotte	3	Nichola	$4\frac{1}{2}$
Alex	2	Imran	4	Sandeep	$4\frac{1}{2}$
Bhuddi	$4\frac{1}{2}$	Cherie	3	Nusrat	$1\frac{1}{2}$
Nina	5	Morag	$5\frac{1}{2}$	Scott	7
Ian	$4\frac{1}{2}$	Jaimeet	5	Khurram	$4\frac{1}{2}$
Chris	$5\frac{1}{2}$	Diego	$3\frac{1}{2}$	Mike	$6\frac{1}{2}$
Kate	$4\frac{1}{2}$	Pritam	4	Mira	2
Alan	5	Nasreen	4	Karen	$2\frac{1}{2}$

a Complete this table of the shoe sizes.

Shoe size	1	$1\frac{1}{2}$	2	$2\frac{1}{2}$	3	$3\frac{1}{2}$	4	$4\frac{1}{2}$	5	$5\frac{1}{2}$	6	$6\frac{1}{2}$	7
Number of children	1	1	2	1	2	3	4	7	3	2	1	2	1

b The median shoe size is ($4\frac{1}{2}$)

c The modal shoe size is ($4\frac{1}{2}$)

Ma 4, Level 4
Handling data
Test 22 Series 2

Representing & interpreting data in equal class intervals

Level Description element [Pupils] group data, where appropriate, in equal class intervals, represent collected data in frequency diagrams and interpret such diagrams.

1 In a competition to see how many items you could fit into a matchbox, these were the results:

```
 7  11  12  15  18  19  15  14  10   6  14  15  20
10   8  11  14  17  18  19  16  14  10   9  17  20
13  20  19  16  17
```

a Complete this tally chart of the data.

Number of items	Tally	Frequency
6 – 8	|||	3
9 – 11	||||| ||	7
12 – 14	|||||		6
15 – 17	||||| ||||	9
18 – 20	||||| |||	8

b Draw a frequency diagram of the results on this grid.

c Complete these statements about the data.

The median is (15)   The mode is (14)

Ma 4, Level 4
Handling data
Test 22 Series 1

Representing & interpreting data in equal class intervals

Level Description element [Pupils] group data, where appropriate, in equal class intervals, represent collected data in frequency diagrams and interpret such diagrams.

1 Tariq made a list of the number of items in the desk or locker of each of his friends.

```
10   8  11  16  11  15  12  11   9  10  11  12  11
 9   8  17  12  10   8  12  17   8  12  17  16  17   9
14  13  12  10   8   8  10  12  16  12   9  14  10
```

a Complete this tally chart of the data.

Number of items	Tally	Frequency
8 – 9	||||| |||	8
10 – 11	||||| |||||		11
12 – 13	||||| ||||	9
14 – 15	||||	4
16 – 17	||||| ||	7

b Draw a frequency diagram of the results on this grid.

c Complete these statements about the data.

The median is (12)   The mode is (12)

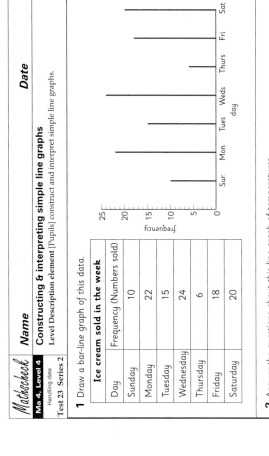
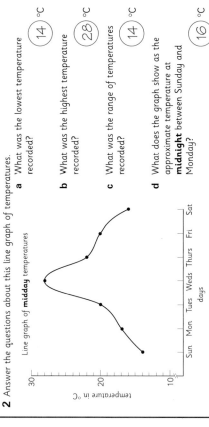

Constructing & interpreting simple line graphs

Ma 4, Level 4
Handling data
Test 23 Series 2

Level Description element [Pupils] construct and interpret simple line graphs.

1 Draw a bar-line graph of this data.

Ice cream sold in the week	
Day	Frequency (Numbers sold)
Sunday	10
Monday	22
Tuesday	15
Wednesday	24
Thursday	6
Friday	18
Saturday	20

2 Answer the questions about this line graph of temperatures.

a What was the lowest temperature recorded? (14) °C

b What was the highest temperature recorded? (28) °C

c What was the range of temperatures recorded? (14) °C

d What does the graph show as the approximate temperature at **midnight** between Sunday and Monday? (16) °C

e Write why this is only a guess at the temperature at midnight.

Readings were taken only at midday so there is no evidence of fluctuations between the recorded times. We can only guess the temperature at midnight by inspection of the line connecting the previous and subsequent midday temperatures.

© HarperCollins Publishers Ltd 1996

Constructing & interpreting simple line graphs

Ma 4, Level 4
Handling data
Test 23 Series 1

Level Description element [Pupils] construct and interpret simple line graphs.

1 Draw a bar-line graph of this data.

Score when rolling a dice 120 times	
Score	Frequency (Number of times)
1	15
2	24
3	20
4	18
5	22
6	21

2 Answer the questions about this line graph of temperatures.

a What was the highest temperature recorded? (29) °C

b What was the lowest temperature recorded? (12) °C

c What was the range of temperatures recorded? (17) °C

d What does the graph show as the approximate temperature at **midnight** between Wednesday and Thursday? (17) °C

e Write why this is only a guess at the temperature at midnight.

Readings were only taken at midday so there is no evidence of fluctuations between the recorded times. We can only guess the temperature at midnight by inspection of the line connecting the previous and subsequent midday temperatures.

© HarperCollins Publishers Ltd 1996

Mathscheck — Test 24 Series 1

Ma 4, Level 4
Handling data
Test 24 Series 1

Probability: certainty & uncertainty, likelihood & fairness
Level Description element [Pupils] understand and use simple vocabulary associated with probability, including 'fair', 'certain' and 'likely'.

Tick the correct word.

1 The day after Friday will be Saturday:
certain ✓
uncertain
impossible

2 It will rain on your birthday:
certain
uncertain ✓
impossible

There may be variations depending on exceptional local or personal circumstances.

3 The first cube you take from the box will be red:
certain
uncertain
impossible ✓

(box containing cubes: blue, blue, blue)

4 You will see a green bike today:
certain
uncertain ✓
impossible

There may be variations depending on exceptional local or personal circumstances.

5 If you roll a die it will score 2:
certain
uncertain ✓
impossible

6 A spider will say your name today:
certain
uncertain
impossible ✓

Mathscheck — Test 24 Series 2

Ma 4, Level 4
Handling data
Test 24 Series 2

Probability: certainty & uncertainty, likelihood & fairness
Level Description element [Pupils] understand and use simple vocabulary associated with probability, including 'fair', 'certain' and 'likely'.

Tick the correct word.

1 You will be 100 years old tomorrow:
certain
uncertain
impossible ✓

2 £1 is more than 1p:
certain ✓
uncertain
impossible

3 It will be salad for tea today:
certain
uncertain ✓
impossible

There may be variations depending on exceptional local or personal circumstances.

4 The first cube you take from the box will be blue:
certain
uncertain ✓
impossible

(box containing cubes: red, green, blue)

5 Today you will meet a dog as tall as your house:
certain
uncertain
impossible ✓

6 You will watch a film about tigers today:
certain
uncertain ✓
impossible

There may be variations depending on exceptional local or personal circumstances.

Sheet 1

Ma 4, Level 4
Handling data
Test 24 Series 1

Probability: certainty & uncertainty, likelihood & fairness

Level Description element [Pupils] understand and use simple vocabulary associated with probability, including 'fair', 'certain' and 'likely'.

7 Are these events **more likely** or **less likely** to happen?
Write 'more' or 'less' in the correct spaces.

(more) likely (less) likely   (less) likely (more) likely

8 A packet of sweets has these numbers of different colours.

Colour	Number
red	15
yellow	2
brown	10
pink	7

I tip out one sweet.
a Which colour am I **most likely** to tip out? (red)
b Write why you chose that colour.

E.g. more reds than any other colour

c Which colour am I **least likely** to tip out? (yellow)

9 Are these events very likely , likely , unlikely or very unlikely to happen?

a You will be in Australia tomorrow. (very unlikely)

Allow for local and personal variations and alternatives.

b It will be icy next winter. (very likely)

c There will be a cartoon on television at 5 o'clock. (likely)

d Someone in your class will have a birthday next month. (likely)

Sheet 2

Ma 4, Level 4
Handling data
Test 24 Series 2

Probability: certainty & uncertainty, likelihood & fairness

Level Description element [Pupils] understand and use simple vocabulary associated with probability, including 'fair', 'certain' and 'likely'.

7 Are these events **more likely** or **less likely** to happen?
Write 'more' or 'less' in the correct spaces.

(less) likely (more) likely   (less) likely (more) likely

8 A box of mixed crayons has these numbers of different colours.

Colour	Number
black	25
green	7
orange	12
blue	19

I close my eyes and pick out one crayon.
a Which colour am I **least likely** to pick out? (green)
b Write why you chose that colour.

E.g. fewer greens than any other colour

c Which colour am I **most likely** to pick out? (black)

9 Are these events very likely , likely , unlikely or very unlikely to happen?

a You will get £100 pocket money next week. (very unlikely)

Allow for local and personal variations and alternatives.

b A new girl will join your class next year. (likely)

c You will find 10p outside school today. (unlikely)

d There will be a cloud in the sky on Monday. (very likely)

124

Mathscheck **Name** — **Date**

Probability: certainty & uncertainty, likelihood & fairness

Level Description element [Pupils] understand and use simple vocabulary associated with probability, including 'fair', 'certain' and 'likely'.

10 Look at this spinner.

After spinning the pointer:
a the **least likely** result is
b the **most likely** result is

draw the patterns

11 Colour these spinners so that the result of a spin:

a is **unlikely** to point to green
b is **certain** to point to blue
c has an **even chance** of pointing to red or yellow

only one or two coloured green — *coloured all blue* — *half coloured red and half coloured yellow*

d is **likely** to point to red
e has **no chance** of pointing to red
f is **equally likely** to point to brown, red and blue

four or five coloured red — *all coloured other than red* — *two coloured red, two coloured brown and two coloured blue*

12 Are these dice games **fair** or **unfair**?

a Tariq has to roll a 6 to win. Sonia has to roll a 1 to win.

b Eric has to roll an even number to win. Lucy has to roll an odd number to win.

write **fair** or **unfair**

fair

fair

Mathscheck **Name** — **Date**

Probability: certainty & uncertainty, likelihood & fairness

Level Description element [Pupils] understand and use simple vocabulary associated with probability, including 'fair', 'certain' and 'likely'.

10 Look at this spinner.

After spinning the pointer:
a the **most likely** result is
b the **least likely** result is

draw the patterns

11 Colour these spinners so that the result of a spin:

a is **likely** to point to blue
b is **certain** to point to red
c has **no chance** of pointing to blue

four or five coloured blue — *coloured all red* — *all coloured other than blue*

d is **unlikely** to point to yellow
e has an **even chance** of pointing to the red or green
f is **equally likely** to score red, blue or yellow

only one or two coloured yellow — *half coloured red and half coloured green* — *two coloured red, two coloured blue and two coloured yellow*

12 Are these dice games **fair** or **unfair**?

a James has to roll 1 or 2 to win. Janet has to roll 5 or 6 to win.

b Mary has to roll an even number to win. Freddie has to roll 1 or 6 to win.

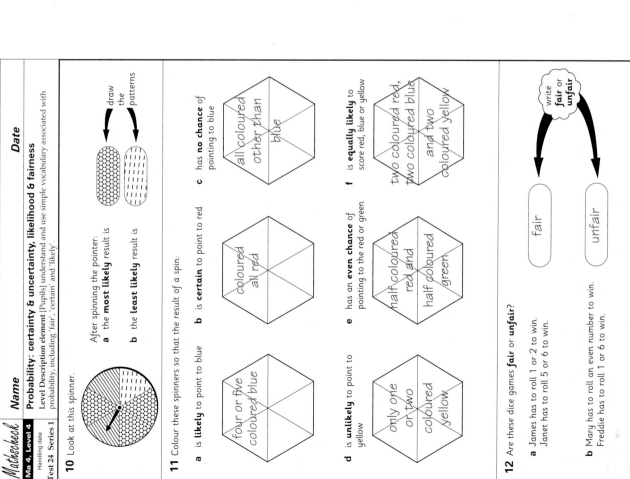

write **fair** or **unfair**

fair

unfair